I'M SO TIRED
OF ACTING SPIRITUAL

Other Books by Melinda Fish

Restoring the Wounded Woman: Recovering from Heartache and Discouragement
Adult Children and the Almighty: Recovering from the Wounds of a Dysfunctional Home
When Addiction Comes to Church: Helping Yourself and Others Move into Recovery

I'm So Tired of Acting Spiritual

Peeling Back the Mask

Melinda Fish

1088
Chosen Books

A Division of Baker Book House Co
Grand Rapids, Michigan 49516

© 1996 by Melinda Fish

Published by Chosen Books
a division of Baker Book House Company
P.O. Box 6287, Grand Rapids, MI 49516-6287

Printed in the United States of America

Library of Congress Cataloging-in-Publication Data

Fish, Melinda.
    I'm so tired of acting spiritual : peeling back the mask / Melinda Fish.
      p. cm.
    Includes bibliographical references (p.).
    ISBN 0-8007-9237-8 (pbk.)
    1. Fanaticism. 2. Religious addiction—Christianity. 3. Spiritual life—Christianity. I. Title.
BR114.F57 1996
248.4—dc20   95-47166

Unless otherwise noted, Scripture quotations are from The New King James Version. Copyright © 1979, 1980, 1982, Thomas Nelson, Inc., Publishers.

Scripture quotations identified NASB are from the New American Standard Bible, copyright © the Lockman Foundation 1960, 1962, 1963, 1968, 1971, 1972, 1973, 1975, 1977.

Scripture quotations identified KJV are from the King James Version of the Bible.

To my brothers and sisters in Christ
at Church of the Risen Saviour
Trafford, Pennsylvania

They think serving God is glorious fun!

CONTENTS

ACKNOWLEDGMENTS

My very special thanks is extended to the following people who, either knowingly or unknowingly, helped me:

My husband, Bill
Ray Alexander
Jane Campbell
The Revs. Jim and Joyce Hart
Sarah Fish and William A. Fish, our children
Patsy Lennon
Leonard and Sandra LeSourd
Sarah Phillips
The Rev. A. J. Rowden and Evangelistic Center Church, Kansas City, Missouri
Diane Sives
Joe and Dorothy Spooner
The Rev. George and Joanne Stockhowe
Kevin and Pam Swadling
Elliott and Mary Tepper
Toronto Airport Vineyard Church, the Rev. John and Carol Arnott, pastors, Etobicoke, Ontario, Guy Chevreau, adjunct teacher
Beverly Watt
Merle Wilson, my mother

IF THE YOKE IS EASY,
WHY AM I SO TIRED?

I f Jesus warned you even once to beware of something, do
you think you should examine it and beware of it? What if
He told you more than thirteen times?

This book is about the trait that angered Jesus most, the
trait He was most concerned would overtake His disciples,
the trait that resulted in His death. It may be the most subtle deception ever to befall a Christian and one of the least
identified and preached-about topics of Christian discipleship: the leaven of the Pharisees.

Let me tell you how it crept into my life.

Lying on our cool concrete driveway early in the morning
when I was a child and gazing at the sky over Angleton, Texas,
I had known I wanted to be a spiritual person—to really know
God. Little did I realize that this desire would catapult me
toward the Lord Jesus Christ, but also down a twenty-year
detour that nearly quenched every ounce of spiritual desire.

In October 1971 while I rode in a car to a women's conference, my close friend, Sarah Phillips, said the sentence that changed my life.

"Did you know that Pat Boone speaks in tongues?" she drawled in her soft Carolina dialect.

Sophisticated people, I had always thought, did not give way to such radical expressions of faith. But there it was—the first sign that a supernatural Lord wants to invade the lives of Christians today with a new sense of His power.

I decided in my heart that if God was doing something in our day, I wanted to be part of it.

I spent the next four months in hot pursuit of the Lord. Sarah and I and two other women formed a weekly prayer group and prepared ourselves for whatever God had for us. As our hunger increased, our frustration did, too, until one by one each of the four of us was touched by the power of the Holy Spirit and set on a course out of apathy and into some form of Christian service. I was filled with a joy I had never experienced.

Within a few months the students in the high school where I taught English began to notice something radically different about me, and actually began to ask me about the Lord. Several of them accepted Christ. There would be no end, I thought, to what the Lord and I could accomplish together!

But at this intersection my spiritual troubles began.

Six months later the joy of being filled with the Holy Spirit had gradually been replaced by numbness. The power of the Holy Spirit that had led me gently seemed to be gone. But knowing that only Jesus was the source of joy, I knew I must now make sure that the once apathetic Melinda stayed dead and buried. I did not know then that I had been infected, in spite of my sincerity, with a religious fungus.

What Jesus called "the leaven of the Pharisees" worked like the silent presence of yeast in a batch of dough. It crept first into my emotions and permeated my spirit until it showed on my countenance. I became stern. Following Christ was serious business. I had no time left for frivolous pursuits like cooking dinner. If Jesus was coming back in my lifetime, I had no time to waste. I had to make sure Jesus found me in a state of perfection.

My prayer life had to develop. I had to lead the lost to Christ. I had to set an example that would funnel those around me into the Kingdom of God. I had to pursue spiritual gifts and hone them into useful tools for God's will for my life. I had to discover and submit to what spiritual leaders called "the dealings of God." I had to mature—fast. And in case others did not notice, I had to look "spiritual."

The Purge

I began a fervent "holy war" against myself. "We've met the enemy and they is us!" was my oft-quoted watchword. As my emotions grew even more numb, I began to search myself for the missing secret to real spirituality. I had to regain a sense of God's presence.

One book I read exposed contraband trinkets around the house as possible sources of a "heavy spirit." Out went the leather stool I had bought in Mexico with the Aztec sun god on it, followed quickly by owl macramés from the '60s and the drum from the Philippines that my mother-in-law had given me with the dragon carvings on it. Dutifully I packed away the TV, to be brought out only for emergencies, such as the rise of the Antichrist.

But buried in my bureau drawers were more enemies of the Gospel: my orange bikini, all my pairs of Bermuda shorts, my earrings and makeup. Out they went with all the fervor I could muster—a small price to pay, I decided, for real spirituality.

I did not notice that I felt less joy than ever.

On to attitudes and doctrines. I read every book on the Christian bookstore shelves about the struggle for faith, miracles and overcoming demonic influences. I overturned my long-held doctrines of "greasy" grace and eternal security. If the truth about the Holy Spirit had been obscured from me, what other scriptural secrets had my denomination failed to report? Perhaps my ignorance of the demonic realm had left me prey and I had unwittingly "picked up" demons along the way or succumbed to familial curses.

Still I did not notice that all my purging did not bring back the joy of His presence.

The pursuit of miracle-working faith captured my attention next. I saw every disappointment as a challenge to the power of my faith. Faith was the key to God's power erupting in my life. Without it I could neither please God nor see the fulfillment of His will. I had to discover its secret and release it to work for me. Perhaps God was teaching me in a wilderness experience and would leave me there until I could master the techniques.

Colds and flu viruses provided choice spiritual battlegrounds. When that achy feeling overtook me, I was thrust into the place of prayer. What sin had I committed that had left the door open for Satan to attack me? Had I succumbed to temptation or doubt? I needed to deny myself more—my feelings, my symptoms. I would let no negative word pass my lips. To say the word *flu* might give over precious, fought-for ground that would result in spiritual defeat. I dreaded days off from work that would let my co-workers know Jesus did not have the power to keep me healthy. I had to be strong. But each time my temperature rose, I knew somehow I had failed to touch God with my faith.

The flu was one thing. Then my fledgling faith failed to obtain God's favor for my father, who had a heart condition, and he died. I struggled for months, inwardly crushed, to hold onto God. To grieve would not, I felt, be an appropriate expression of faith. I was supposed to feel, after all, that He was in control. But sometimes at night my humanity got the best of me and I cried myself to sleep, wondering where God was and what I had done wrong.

Around this time I encountered the most spiritual women I had ever met. These were not the typically benign ladies like the ones in the church where I grew up who brought over a casserole when you were sick. These were spiritual superwomen. Their mode of dress and way of speech added a dramatic flair to the simplicity of the Gospel. When they prayed at the altar, their voices rose and fell with crescendos of emotion. They found insightful passages in books like Habakkuk and saw hidden meanings seemingly obscured from even the pastor. They spent hours in prayer and days in fasting. They were sought out by others for counseling and prayer.

I knew these women were on the cutting edge of what God was doing and I wanted to be like them. When they went to the altar, I went, too, even if I felt nothing. I made myself aware of how they were praying. I emulated their intensity and stirring of tears. Attaching myself to them, I secretly hoped to be known as one of the spiritually elite. I took every bit of their counsel to heart and assimilated it into my life.

But everything was hard. Not once did I allow myself to think that Jesus was not in all this whirlwind. He had to be. These women were obviously hungrier for God and more gifted than I was.

But following God remained a struggle. I was tired. Staying "spiritual" was difficult, and I did not know I was striving under a self-inflicted load that was actually quenching the Holy Spirit in my life. It took years to develop the courage to drop out of the race, to find the real me behind the mask and begin a journey in the easy yoke of Christ.

What about You?

In almost every place I have been since then, I have seen sincere Christians like me struggling to obtain or maintain the seal of God's favor on their lives. Perhaps you or someone you know is stumbling under the weight of a false yoke, thinking it is the weight of the cross. Many Christians pass through a phase in their spiritual development in which zeal exceeds the gentle leading of the Holy Spirit.

But some become stuck in this phase, cycling through a series of attempts to conform to an unwritten, self-imposed standard they believe to be true spirituality. In so doing they not only stunt their own spiritual growth but repel unbelievers from the Lord and hurt other Christians, doing damage to the local church. Even worse, this phase has the power to turn a sincere Christian into a self-styled zealot who, even out of sincerity, can miss the best that a relationship with Jesus has to offer and wind up quenching the power of the Holy Spirit in his or her own life and the lives of others. Rather than promoting the work of God, such a spiritual zealot can actually wind up opposing the revival he himself has prayed for and missing the move of the Holy Spirit in the Church in his generation.

Perhaps someone you know has been smitten with this syndrome. We find these people in the pulpits and the pews. They appear spiritually strong but do not live in the spiritual realm they claim to have achieved. Some call it "superspirituality," but it is not spiritual. In fact, it is nothing close to what Jesus considered spiritual. Instead, it is religiosity born of sincerity and deep emotional need. Such a Christian, if allowed to proceed, will grow not into the image of Christ but into the image of a Pharisee.

Many fellow believers cannot discern the difference. They may admire "superspiritual" Christians and be fooled temporarily by their demeanors, not knowing they are hollow emotionally and devoid of joy, set up to sin against themselves, God and others. What they need most are brothers and sisters who, courageously and lovingly, refuse to play along but help puncture their denial and point them lovingly to the freedom of childlike faith in their heavenly Father.

If *you* are infected, you may already have felt uncomfortable reading this chapter. I double-dare you to read on. You believe it is impossible to be too spiritual. This is true, but it *is* possible to substitute the false for the real and wake up one day in bondage—or, worse, never wake up to the fact that you have impressed people while unintentionally grieving the Holy Spirit.

This book is for the Christian who is tired of acting "spiritual," who wants to peel back the mask and get real. You are looking for divine permission. You are sick of trying to please God with spiritual discipline as your joy ebbs away.

Where are the people who admit that straining does not produce faith? Where are the Christians who admire Christlike character rather than sensationalism? You are wondering if you can be a "normal" person and still have God's unconditional love. Perhaps you are tired of being controlled by the spiritually intimidating and wonder if anyone sees false spirituality for what it is. Or maybe your spiritual life has reached a place of deep regret where you shudder at your own mistakes.

As you read in this book about the battles of other Christians, I hope you will see the humor and futility in our struggles to be who we are not. Maybe then you can relax and bask in the love of God and come to actually enjoy being a Christian.

Is false spirituality readily discernible? It wasn't for me. Take a pencil and answer the following questions *yes* or *no:*

_____ 1. I really enjoy praying.
_____ 2. I often feel numb emotionally even though I feel I must be strong spiritually.
_____ 3. Sometimes I feel that if I express doubt or fear, God will be displeased, and negative circumstances may occur outside of His will.
_____ 4. When a negative event or series of events occurs in my life, I tend to feel I have neglected some area of

Christian discipline such as prayer, Bible study or tithing.

_____ 5. I feel intimidated by more "spiritual" believers.

_____ 6. I feel that if I let down my guard, I will not fulfill God's purpose for my life.

_____ 7. If I testify about the blessing of the Lord in some area of my life, I will likely be attacked by Satan.

_____ 8. If I fail to pray intensely, God will not hear me or answer my prayer.

_____ 9. Sometimes I feel secretly that I am more obedient to the Lord than those around me who are less gifted or less disciplined spiritually.

_____10. I admire only those Christians who are serious about seeking the Lord continuously.

_____11. Talking for very long about everyday issues of life makes me feel uncomfortable, as though the world is becoming too important to me.

_____12. Laughter has little or no place in the life of a person who is serious about following Christ.

_____13. There have been times when I wanted people to know how long I prayed and how much I fasted.

_____14. I am afraid to want anything for fear it may not be the will of God.

_____15. I know God will always love and approve of me no matter what happens.

Check to see how many *yes* answers you gave. *Yes* to numbers 2–14 and *no* to numbers 1 and 15 indicate that your spiritual life is degenerating to "code blue." You have the right book in your hands!

Let's begin our journey by peeling back the religious mask.

2

WHEN PHARISEES COME TO CHURCH

B y the time Bill and I had pastored an inner-city church
for ten years, I had my spiritual mask perfected and com-
fortably in place. The problem was, I did not know I was
wearing a mask until something happened to crack my denial system.

No longer did I expect to experience joy because the ministry had become such a struggle. But in spite of our leaky
rented building and lack of other seeker-sensitive necessities,
like a music program and adequate heat, we did have a congregation on Sundays of around 120 faithful. These included
street people and patients with weekend passes from the St.
Francis Hospital psychiatric ward. Those who came seemed
not to mind that some Sundays the water in the toilets had
frozen or that a large rat had found its home in our church
kitchen and darted across the back of the church during the
services. A closely knit congregation, we were convinced our
heartfelt prayers for revival would soon be answered.

Revival had been the focus of our praying for several years. We sought the Lord earnestly for it during four services per week. In order to obtain revival, which I believed the responsibility of leadership, I impressed on my husband the need to fast and pray.

And fast we did. The spiritual superwomen with whom I had associated taught that fasting held the key to effective prayer. It was the only way to let God know you really meant business. I had read extensively on the subject and was convinced that but for a few more missed meals, revival would fall on our church.

A repentant heart, of course, had to lie underneath it all. The books I had read on revivals of the past cited examples of visitations that had been withheld due to unconfessed sin, no matter how slight, until a tiny remnant had been earnest enough to prevail with God. So I followed their example, recalling to the Lord everything—from pride all the way to the gum wrapper I had thrown on the sidewalk the previous week—that might blight my conscience.

Months wore into years. By this time I was outstripping every Christian I knew or had ever read about in the fasting department, including Moses and Jesus. I had fasted many times for three-day intervals. When this did not do it, I escalated to seven-day intervals. I gutted out a 21-day and even a forty-day fast. All I got was hunger and secret pride in myself—but no revival.

At least no one could fault me for not having sought God with a whole heart.

Dirk

About this time a young man in his early twenties, whom I will call Dirk, joined our congregation. Dirk was coming back to the Lord after a two-year period of backsliding into drugs and immorality. He dropped out of college to live in the church and help with the building maintenance. We embraced him into our fellowship and quickly became impressed with his devotion to the Lord.

Dirk gave himself willingly and ceaselessly to help the elderly in the congregation and the street people who happened by the church building during the week. He even began a weekly prayer group on Friday nights to seek God for revival. We welcomed his help because by this time we were exhausted from our frenzied pace of seeking God. (I had begun to experience severe stomach pain.) Dirk shared frequent testimonies and began devoting himself to extensive periods of prayer and fasting. Sometimes we were afraid Dirk was doing too much, but we knew how important it was to seek God, so we said little to him other than exhorting him not to overdo it.

Slowly Dirk's zeal began to drive him in a different direction. One Friday night, while Bill worked on his message in his study, I attended the prayer meeting Dirk led. I was happy to see several young men and women engaged in earnest prayer, actually lying prostrate on the floor. But as the meeting wore on, I realized a driving force had taken over. Everyone prayed loudly, but when I tried to pray, I was immediately drowned out—not once but several times.

In the weeks that followed, Dirk began using spiritual gifts to exhort the congregation to repent from apathy. His tone was harsh, almost cruel. He refused to attend the weekly Bible study, praying instead in another part of the building. He became less cooperative and more rebellious. And it was clear his opinion of Bill and me had changed. We were not spiritual enough, in his opinion, to lead the congregation.

One Sunday morning Dirk "prophesied" that if Bill and I did not repent, our ministries would be torn down and God would raise up new leadership that was faithful. The congregation looked stunned; his words stung with judgment. But he said he had to speak out or he would be disobeying

God. I knew how he felt. I, too, had felt driven from time to time to give difficult words of prophecy.

Within a few short weeks, Dirk resisted any attempts by Bill or me or the other church leaders to reconcile. He felt he would be compromising. As members began to leave the church, the gossip intensified.

Then, in a meeting in which the members of Dirk's prayer group were invited to reconcile or to discuss their feelings, one by one they presented a united front of resistance. Dirk said, "You'll have to disfellowship me," indicating he wanted to be "martyred" for the cause.

When the dust settled, our congregation had lost half its members. Had it not been for the influence of two friends in the ministry who visited some of the members tottering on the brink, we would have lost more.

Dirk went on to repeat the scenario in at least two other congregations in the city. Each time he gained influence initially with the pastor and leaders, who did not discern, as Bill and I had not, the difference between true and false spirituality.

Recognizing Leaven

This is the power of the leaven of the Pharisees.

It was no coincidence that caused Jesus to use the word *leaven* to describe what happens to people like Dirk and me. Yeast is actually a fungus that reproduces itself quickly in a warm, moist environment like bread dough. When yeast is activated, it gives off a tantalizing aroma that attracts people to the kitchen to see what is in the oven. Yeast cannot be seen without a microscope, but its effects can be. Once it is introduced into the dough, it takes only an hour before it has enlarged the lump of dough to two or three times its original size. The dough has to be literally punched with a human fist to expel the air so it can rise again before baking.

The apostle Paul used the word *leaven* to describe sin and its effects on the Body of Christ. Jesus used it to describe the effect of false spirituality in the life of an otherwise sincere person. This kind of leaven, once introduced into the receptive environment of the spiritually active Christian, puffs up the believer's head to two or three times its normal size, causing him to "think of [himself] more highly than [he] ought" (Romans 12:3). Its enticing odor attracts many Christians who want to believe there is a realm of spirituality within the reach of only a dynamic few. It makes the believer pray more intensely, fast more often, read the Bible more diligently. Under the influence of this kind of leaven, he or she will act "spiritual" and perform religious functions with alacrity.

But most of this leaven, like a risen mound of bread dough, is hot air that needs to be expelled. It is false spiritual growth that spreads—first in a believer, then in a church or religious group—because no one wants to admit it is there. And this leaven is a cloak for rebellion.

In the weeks that followed the church split, I was miserable. Not only was I heartbroken over what had happened to our church, but I felt helpless, unable to convince Dirk we really did love both God and him. The harder we tried, the more adamantly he had believed we were the enemy.

What bothered me most was that when I really looked at what had happened to Dirk, it felt like looking in a mirror. Where had Dirk gotten the idea that his obsessive praying and fasting were what God wanted from him? How did he come to use spiritual gifts to tear apart rather than build up the local church? Where did he learn that volume equaled anointing? Had it been from me?

It was as if a giant, gentle fist had knocked the wind out of me.

The Making of a Pharisee

Pharisaism appeared first on the scrolls of Jewish history more than one hundred years before Jesus was born. The Pharisees were a sincere party of men whose only desire originally had been to return Israel to faith in the God of the Scriptures. Keeping the Law stood foremost in their doctrine because they believed this would ensure God's favor and prevent His judgment. We would find their beliefs similar to the tenets of faith held by the majority of evangelical Christians today.

Pharisees believed, for example, in the authority of the Scriptures and in committing passages to memory. They tithed fastidiously. They adhered to supernatural elements of the faith like the resurrection of the dead and casting out demons. They believed in passing on godly traditions to their children and converting others to faith in the Lord. Personal holiness of heart and life that would separate them from the world was the doctrine that gave them the name *Pharisee,* derived from a Hebrew word meaning "separate." These were earnest people who cared that things were done well.

But by the time Jesus came, the sect of the Pharisees had left its humble beginnings and become a force that wielded both religious and political power often greater than that of priests and kings. They had developed a religious system that defined for every Jewish person what it meant to be truly spiritual. And they were feared by the masses. Certain infringements of Jewish law, such as heresy, were punishable by death, and people feared the Pharisees as merciless men who could influence the governing powers to convict and execute the average man. Sadly, they never realized their sincerity would oppose the God they were trying to honor.

The spirit of Pharisaism lives today in Christianity. It overwhelms sincere Christians who come to Jesus Christ but never allow Him to touch some of their deepest emotional wounds. Those who are most vulnerable need to prove to themselves, God and others that they are worthy of His love. As they step onto this never-ending treadmill of performance-based Christianity, they lose sight of the grace of God and become frustrated. Failing to find the approval of God, they derive satisfaction from making others adhere to their own rigid standard of spirituality.

Dirk came into our church after a period of backsliding into drugs and immorality. His family had no use for God or the Church. Nor were they very affectionate. Dirk had difficulty finding direction for his life and often looked for jobs that paid quick money. Although he was very capable, he dropped out of college. His father, a wealthy executive, was usually consumed with his work and disapproved of Dirk's aimlessness. Excelling spiritually was the only way Dirk could validate his existence.

I, too, had deep emotional needs that made me vulnerable to the leaven of the Pharisees. The older of two children, I hungered for and thrived on approval from others. In fact, I felt I needed approval to survive. Although I remember my small-town childhood as secure and happy, I felt unsure of myself. I was never part of the "in" crowd at school. I suppose I felt average, and to me average has always meant inferior. I remember making up my mind to be someone who would make a difference. Later, when my high school class voted me "Most Likely to Succeed," I had a goal to meet: success. More than that, I wanted never again to feel socially unacceptable. So when the Body of Christ became my peers, I developed a mask.

The Spiritual Mask

The "Pharisees" in the Body of Christ always wear masks that separate them from the average Christian. But under every religious mask, even the most intimidating one, is a person who needs to feel God's unconditional love. The mask-wearer has felt inferior and, in his or her normal state, unacceptable to God and others. Perhaps he has recognized that his faith is weak or that his natural personality does not meet others' standards of spirituality. Maybe his life falls short of spiritual "correctness" in some important area and he feels embarrassed that all his efforts have not produced spiritual fruit. In order to be respected and loved, he feels he must be someone else. After all, the way he is now must displease God or his prayers would be answered.

If emotional needs are left unmet, the unwary Christian will inevitably seek other ways to fill them. When insecurity festers, he will try to feel significant by overcompensating in some area of talent, or by shaping a religious mask to cover his sense of shame. Because his emotional needs have not been filled by others, he tends not to trust people. He often becomes suspicious and hypervigilant, seeking to discover impure motives in those around him. And to protect himself, he must be in control. This leads to rebellion against God and authority, which he will excuse, even though he knows rebellion is unacceptable for a Christian, by claiming a deeper mandate from God that supersedes the need to cooperate with the group.

The Pharisees themselves, establishing their own brand of righteousness, did not submit to God for cleansing from sin. Instead they broadened their phylacteries, lengthened the tassels of their prayer shawls, sought respectful greetings in the marketplace and used other externals as a religious cloak for their rebellion. They neglected what was important to God—love, justice, mercy and truth—to focus on details of lesser importance. Finally they attempted to destroy the Messiah, for whom they had waited for centuries, because He did not fit their definition of a Messiah. Their religious masks separated them not merely from the masses, but ultimately from God.

The Scriptures talk about dramatic changes that occur in a believer in Christ when the Holy Spirit enters his or her life. God promises to make all things new and to transform us from glory to glory into the image of Christ. But the kinds of changes the Bible talks about take years of walking with Christ—sometimes even a lifetime.

Then there is counterfeit change. Human beings are born mimics. We tend to live out behavior and even mannerisms that are modeled by others we love and respect. Since we cannot see Jesus now, we imagine what He must be like. Rather than wait for the Holy Spirit to transform us gradually into the character of Jesus, we may prefer to use our concept of what Jesus is like and act it out. Hollywood, unfortunately, has fleshed out an image of Jesus that sticks in the mind of many Christians. To the Hollywood director, Jesus is somber, zombie-like, dramatic and usually glows in the dark.

But it may not be Hollywood that sets the model of superspirituality for the impressionable Christian. It may be someone we feel lives a little closer to God than we do. We emulate his or her vocal inflection in prayer. The insecure person called upon to give a devotional hears the voice of the person he is emulating resounding in his head more loudly than his own. Without even realizing it, he winds up transforming himself into a replica of someone else.

Not just the insecure individual is guilty of this. Unfortunately, the Body of Christ has adopted certain demeanors to which we respond as "spiritual"—the resonant, dramatic voice of the evangelical TV pastor; the animated, dynamic delivery of the Pentecostal evangelist; the ceremoniously poised presence of the Pope. The Church has developed traditions into which we feel we must fit if we are to be accepted as having anything worthy to say to the Body of Christ.

Often it is not what is said but *how* it is said that determines its acceptance. One evening while channel surfing, I ran across a comedy program. Jesse Jackson, the politician/preacher, was perched in front of a stained-glass window reading Dr. Seuss in his preaching voice: "I will not eat-uh, green eggs and ham-uh, I will not eat them, Sam, I am-uh. . . ." Had Jackson been reading that story to a church crowd instead of a TV audience, some might have leapt to their feet and praised the Lord. It was the tone of his voice, not his words, that punched the praise button.

So what happens if you know God is calling you into the ministry but you perceive yourself as a lackluster orator incapable of stirring a crowd? Developing a dynamic presence can mean the difference between a call to "First Church, Big City" or pastoring "the little brown church in the vale." All too often pulpit committees are swayed by externals. No one wants a normal man in the pulpit. The prospective minister knows he must look and act spiritual and be someone who meets all our needs as Jesus would meet them. He knows we want someone who lives in that realm we all believe exists: hyperspirituality.

Shaping the Mask

Every person who tries to take the shortcut approach (regardless of the model) to spirituality adopts a mask and wears it so much that soon even he cannot tell the difference between himself and the facade. The mask involves every part of life, from dress to doctrine.

The development of a religious mask always involves some external mark that sets the wearer apart to be noticed by others. Certain looks are considered spiritual in various religious circles, whether it is the church that "dresses for success," the one that sets its spiritually elite apart with religious vestments or the one that takes pride in dressing so casually that its members make John the Baptist look like a fashion maven. While I felt more spiritual dressing for success, Dirk adopted the John the Baptist look. He grew out his beard and refused to dress for church in anything other than jeans and a plaid flannel shirt. It became his uniform.

Does God really care that much? The question we must answer is, Does this way of dressing make me feel more acceptable to God or more noticeable to others by setting me apart from the group? The reply can provide a warning.

But doesn't the Lord care about externals at all?

When the Holy Spirit began working on me, I knew He was conforming me to a new internal standard of modesty. The orange bikini had to go. I felt uncomfortable, even ashamed, wearing it (although I know some Christians do not share this conviction). Fortunately for the viewing public, I have never wanted to buy another.

But I did not stop where the Holy Spirit stopped. I had also heard that some of the spiritual superwomen had been convicted about wearing makeup and earrings. One minister friend of ours pointed out regularly that the word *cosmetic* comes from the word *cosmos,* which means "world." Cosmetics, he said, obscured the glory of Christ on a woman's countenance.

Not wanting to be perceived as unholy and rebellious, and certainly not wanting to be worldly, I listened. Hoping everyone would see the absence of lipstick on me as the unmistakable sign of the presence of God and quickly pant for more of the Lord, I discarded every article of makeup and let my hair grow out. I never bothered to ask Bill what he thought about it. Not until two years later (after I had backslidden into a Mary Kay party) did I realize he liked me with makeup on.

Giving up makeup and earrings are tokens of the self-denial that is always part of the religious mask. Self-denial is a step toward self-martyrdom—another factor always present in the superspiritual Christian. Since martyrdom is the ultimate act of spirituality, the person who tries to portray himself as spiritual must display tokens of his willingness to suffer for the Gospel. He must follow Jesus with a moroseness that lets the world know how sincere he is. We can often see on his face degrees of seriousness characterized by what psychologists call a sad affect or countenance. Photographs taken of me during the era of my superspiritual mode show me as pale, somber, devoid of joy.

Throwing one's life down for spiritual causes is essential to prove the super-Christian's devotion to the higher spiritual realm. Instead of waiting for Jesus to lead him or her at the moment of His choosing through the valley of the shadow of death, the Pharisee presses toward it, sometimes with foolish acts of self-denial. He may leave a job to prove his spirituality or choose the hardest mission opportunity— not because Jesus is leading him, but because his concept of God as a stern taskmaster controls his actions.

Ironically, pride, not spirituality, authors these acts. Paul alluded to this when he wrote: "Though I bestow all my goods to feed the poor, and though I give my body to be burned, but have not love, it profits me nothing" (1 Corinthians 13:3).

Saying what is spiritually "correct" in each situation, when developing your spiritual image, is as important as dressing the part. When I was first filled with the Holy Spirit, I wanted to talk about nothing other than the Lord, the Word and the Church. The Holy Spirit had rearranged my priorities and I could not help but vocalize my enthusiasm. But when my joy helped to attract several students in my high school English classes, as well as several acquaintances, to the Lord, I resolved to speak of nothing except spiritual matters. Time was running out, after all, and to talk of the mundane was idle—foolishness I would have to account for in the Judgment that I prepared myself constantly to face.

So I sprinkled every conversation liberally with references to the Lord. Hoping the irreligious would hear some convicting tidbit and be drawn to Him, I punctuated everything with phrases like "Praise the Lord!" to let them know where I stood. In Christian circles I directed each conversation into reflection on what the Lord might consider important. I felt led to address every issue with Bible references, chapter and verse, and allowed not a single errant view to escape without challenge. Deep down I wanted to be a leader, which drove me to acts of "obedience" that would set me apart from average Christians.

During this time the spiritual superfolks discovered the gift of prophecy. Soon it became the mark of spirituality to be a conveyor of "words" from God to individuals. The genuine gift of prophecy, of course, strengthens the Body of Christ. But my doctrine of holiness had begun to be turned subtly into a works theology (although I would have never used the word *works* to describe it). My concept of God had become frightening; anything coming through me anymore had the tone of conditional love. Any blessings promised had contingencies attached that would invalidate the blessings unless the believers behaved themselves. There was an intensity about the Bible studies I taught—an intensity I thought came from the heart of God. Even more disturbing was that people loved it—except for the Presbyterian minister I "victimized" with one of my so-called "words from God."

He seemed quite happy, I had noticed, not to adopt any of the trappings of spirituality I had come to admire. His lack of intensity bothered me. A strong voice seemed to be telling me that this minister's compromising had grieved the Holy Spirit, and that if he did not repent, he would not enjoy his upcoming retirement. When I checked this word with the "groupies" I had accumulated who confirmed everything I said as the prophetic voice for the hour, they affirmed me. Not wanting to disobey God, I made an appointment with the minister to warn him.

It makes me cringe today to think of how I must have startled him. After I rattled off the "word," he thanked me graciously, adding that he did not understand the meaning but that he would pray about it. I could not allow myself the luxury of thinking much about how my "word" might affect him. I could not be dissuaded from obedience to God.

It never occurred to me that my "word" was not God but my personal appraisal. Judging people had become a habit. I took everyone's spiritual temperature continually with my thermometer, my standard of spirituality. I allowed as close friends only those who conformed to my doctrines; the others had to be content with life outside my inner circle. I could not allow myself to be tainted with less spiritual believers who might drag me down.

Likewise, Dirk amassed to himself a small congregation within the congregation. He curried the respect of vulnerable young women who considered him extremely spiritual. He made sure they noticed how long he fasted and how well he could discern lukewarmness in others. On one occasion he raced out of a church meeting to a nearby restaurant owned by a family that had started attending the church. He rebuked them severely for some infringement of his own standard of holiness, threatening them with business failure if they did not heed his warning. In retrospect I wonder if he was copying my pattern.

Gradually I came to believe that a realm of spirituality was reserved only for those who would "press in" to it. I thrived on teachings from speakers who taught about "life behind the veil." Somehow the simple Christian believer did not have access to a secret place in God reserved for those whose consecration levels were higher and more devoted. If such a secret life existed, I was determined to find it. I did not want to arrive at the judgment seat and find myself lacking.

I did not know I was biting into the same fruit handed Eve in the Garden. I could not hear, behind the promise of spiritual depth, the voice of temptation moving me from the simplicity of the Gospel of Jesus Christ and into what was really a belief in superior revelation. Forgetting that Jesus came to make God more accessible, I began to believe God was more *in*accessible than anyone imagined. In order to trek boldly into spiritual hyperspace, I knew separation was the key. The false doctrine of perfectionism fed into my need to excel, making me more and more isolated, less and less able to be corrected. No one was spiritual enough, in my opinion, to challenge me.

Buildup for a Fall

A crash was inevitable. I grew tired and knew something was desperately wrong. I could no longer chalk up all the conflict in my life to persecution at the hands of the less spiritual (or another form of satanic attack). On the one hand, I was afraid to look at my self-engendered isolation from the mainstream of the Body of Christ. I had sought the place I had been led to believe existed—life behind the veil, the place few believers ever reach. On the other hand, I had begun to wonder how much more it would cost me to venture into this uncharted sector. I was numb emotionally and nagged by Scripture passages about grace, love and rest. And I had to submit to medical tests for the stomach pain.

Unless people wearing a pharisaical mask experience a severe enough challenge, they never learn. But if the challenge is orchestrated by the Master Teacher, it will begin to peel back the mask. A few of my friends had challenged some of my ideas, but knowing they did not fast and pray as much as I did, I discarded their viewpoints. They simply did not want to pay the price, I thought, to seek God. I could not listen to anyone who was not living in the elite realm of the superspiritual.

Unless I was victimized by someone like me, I might never have seen that the motivating force behind my striving was evil. But the experience with Dirk precipitated the peeling back of my mask. What happened to him, happened to me. Like me, he had become isolated. He had come to believe in a form of spirituality that was a religious cloak for rebellion. The deception was so powerful that no amount of convincing could bring him to admit he was acting out of anything but obedience to the Lord. Such is the power of the religious mask. It is shaped in denial.

Seeing what had happened to Dirk frightened me back to my senses. And once my denial was shattered, the healing power of Jesus Christ began to lead me back.

But before I talk about that, and now that we have looked at the mask of modern-day Pharisaism, let's look at the spirit that drives the person who wears it.

THE DRIVING SPIRIT

Sheep are led, not driven, to the quiet green pastures where they are nurtured. But a butcher who gains control of the flock forces them to market, where their lives are taken from them and their bodies cut apart and sold as products to the highest bidder.

If Satan, the thief and killer of our souls, cannot have us, he will simply resort to pushing us too far. While he shoves some unwary Christians toward apathy, he forces others down a destructive path of overzealousness in order to burn them out. Once their enthusiasm for the Lord is spent, he heaps discouragement and cynicism on them, rendering them of little use to the Kingdom of God. Rather than become living sacrifices for Jesus Christ, they become lifeless, butchered carcasses.

The Bible never identifies zeal as one of the gifts or fruit of the Holy Spirit in our lives. Apparently God knows that everything He wants to accomplish in your life will happen if you simply yield to His presence within you over a lifetime. But fleshly zeal and its accompanying intensity can produce counterfeit fruit. Zeal causes a Christian to move away from enjoying a relationship with Jesus Christ and toward immersion in religious activity. Paul warned the believers that the Law of Moses had given Israel a fleshly zeal without real spiritual knowledge (see Romans 10:2). When any believer substitutes zealousness for the things of God for the joy of a relationship with Him, he or she gives up grace for religious activity.

Here is why zeal fails: It appeals to the fleshly nature of human beings, which seeks to gain the ascendancy in a believer's life. It appeals to basic urges to control oneself and one's environment. Zeal is one of the tools humans use to achieve their goal of survival. Natural survival depends on effort, while survival in the spiritual economy rests in the hands of God. Zeal actually interferes with the formation of godly qualities, which come only through a lifetime of faith and patience. Resorting to natural means to achieve spiritual ends always leads us away from God's best.

Usually the unwary Christian cannot see how his eagerness to serve God is being tainted by the leaven of the Pharisees. In fact, he may believe he is behaving in a Christlike manner and that others around him are the Pharisees for trying to quench his zeal. The deception is powerful and it usually takes more than trying to reason with him to crack it. Some have even called this phenomenon a religious spirit because of its destructive results. Indeed, we should not be ignorant of the fact that Satan is at work.

How Do We Tell the Difference?

Let's look at two qualities that set zeal apart from real spirituality.

The Desire to Ascend

Dirk, the misguided young man in the last chapter, was content initially to serve God and others in the church. But soon he developed a driving desire to gain a place of influence. Eager for God to use him and convinced that those around him needed to be more on fire for God, Dirk began to push. His desire to become a leader drove him to bypass Christ's model of ministry preparation. Instead he wound up choosing a pattern similar to the one Satan chose when he rebelled against God.

The prophet Isaiah described the thoughts that were in Lucifer's heart before God cast him out of heaven: "I will ascend into heaven, I will exalt my throne above the stars of God; . . . I will ascend above the heights of the clouds, I will be like the Most High. . ." (Isaiah 14:13–14).

Paul noticed zealousness in the early Christians pursuing the gifts of the Holy Spirit, and encouraged the believers to "desire spiritual gifts" (1 Corinthians 14:1) and aspire to leadership.

The path we choose to get there, however, spells the difference between arriving and falling by the wayside. Jesus' pathway to influence and leadership was lined with humility. His idea of humility meant losing Himself in the will of God, accepting responsibility and taking a low seat of servanthood. The pathway to power, so far as Jesus was concerned, lay not up but down. He told two of His disciples who wanted to sit on thrones beside Him in His Kingdom that only the Father could grant that request. If they aspired to such thrones, they would have to undergo a baptism of suffering.

The pathway to being used by God leads through years of anonymous servanthood while He brings you to a place of contentment just knowing Him and enjoying a relationship with Him. The pathway leads through testings, such as being passed over while others are blessed, and learning to be truly happy for others who receive what you wanted most.

The pathway to godly leadership requires that you submit to God's time frame, which is usually much longer than ours. This is because character development is primary in God's eyes. He can raise anyone to leadership overnight if He chooses; He did so with Joseph in the Old Testament. But He usually lets that person spend some time in "jail." This deals a death blow to pride.

Using Carnal Methods

The new believer is usually too eager to be in a leadership position, thinking it will soothe his suffering ego. During this time he is tempted to take a shortcut to power. He finds himself struggling to attain.

But power struggle is Satan's domain. He authored the first power struggle, attempting to push God off His throne. Anytime anyone seeks to usurp authority in any arena, religious or political, Satan joins the party and pressures the combatants to resort to carnal methods to achieve spiritual goals. Paul warned the early Church that her weapons were not carnal but divinely powerful to damage Satan's camp (see 2 Corinthians 10:4).

Dirk possessed great potential as a leader, but his grasping for position caused him to disqualify himself. He attempted to push his way in, using even spiritual gifts to help achieve his goals. While the proper use of spiritual gifts builds up the Body of Christ, Dirk used the gifts, especially his own brand of prophecy, to draw attention to himself rather than to Jesus Christ, and ended up tearing the Body of Christ down. His own agenda could be detected at the heart of each manifestation.

Initially Dirk's "prophecies" stirred the congregation, but gradually they began to warn them that things were wrong. Then Dirk began to imply in these prophecies that the congregation and leaders needed to repent. This cast doubt on the leadership. A force drove the congregation to draw battle lines and prepare for war—a false division, since Dirk sought to lead a group of his own. Rather than start a church from the ground up, he sought to sneak into a position of influence and draw sheep away to himself. Dirk's choice of the shortcut to leadership was actually rebellion and manifested far-reaching destructive results to his own life and the spiritual lives of those he led astray.

Dirk is not the only one to attempt such a shortcut to leadership. It happens throughout every sector of the Body of Christ, including in churches that do not practice the use of spiritual gifts. The result is the same: division and the loss of many sheep who become disgusted with the hypocrisy of that church and never again darken its doors.

Rather than allow the Lord to make him truly humble, Dirk used false humility to "prove" his qualification for leadership. False humility is the carnal substitute for the real thing. Bypassing years of character development, a person can resort to a mask of false humility to replace what is missing in his character. He becomes the author of his own salvation and spiritual development. In his blindness to true Christlike qualities, he imitates his own idea of spirituality and begins to do what Paul warned the Colossians against— "taking delight in false humility." Why, Paul asked,

> as though living in the world, do you subject yourselves to regulations—"Do not touch, do not taste, do not handle". . . ? These things indeed have an appearance of wisdom in self-imposed religion, false humility, and neglect of the body, but are of no value against the indulgence of the flesh.
>
> Colossians 2:20–21, 23

Self-abasement robs you of your freedom from legalism. It replaces love for Jesus Christ and others with severe treatment of the body. It makes you take pride in your ability to discipline yourself harshly. Letting God have His way in my life is more unnerving. What if He were to ask me to love someone unlovable or do something not on my agenda? Easier to substitute self-abasement. What if He asked me to give a love offering of money I was planning to spend on something else? I can always give a bigger amount to another cause later and still feel good about myself. Or perhaps I can fast for a week instead.

Self-abasement is a cheaper form of martyrdom. Framed in psychological terms, it has symptoms of masochism—self-punishment. All pagan religions thrive on forms of self-abasement, which include everything from fasting and personal sacrifice to other forms of penance. It is born out of fear—anger at yourself and others and demands that you punish yourself to make up for some sin or spiritual lack. The asceticism of monks, the self-flagellation of pagan religious rites, obsession with spiritual disciplines, vegetarianism, self-deprivation to prove yourself godly or more cosmically aware—all these are substitutes for allowing God to teach you the lessons He knows you need through the circumstances of your life to bring you into Christlikeness.

His lessons can be hard but include happy blessings and are custom-designed to produce true humility, love, joy, peace, patience and the other fruit of the Spirit (see Galatians 5:22–23). These cannot be imitated. They are like precious jewels formed out of the pressures of living; and to meet a person with the real gems is to meet Jesus Christ in another person. You wonder, meeting that person, how you ever could have been deceived by the false.

The Driving Spirit in My Life

In my early zeal, my abuse of fasting became a form of self-abasement. I felt driven by a low sense of self-esteem to punish myself for not being spiritual enough to obtain revival. I began depriving myself of food for days and weeks.

After several days on a long fast, you cease to be aware of hunger as your digestive system shuts down. You actually experience a sense of well-being, a "high," which is further fed by your hopes of spiritual advancement.

Whenever I was fasting, this high made me feel I was *doing* something, rather than just sitting there, while others seemed not to care whether we had revival or not. Responding to the apathy around me, I developed pride— which is at the root of everything we will examine in this book. Rather than becoming more patient with others and esteeming them as better than myself, I became convinced I was in that realm of believers set apart for the highest purposes of God.

Nauseating! But this thought led me to believe I was entitled to the privilege of judging others. Like the Pharisees, I had taken the seat of Moses (see Matthew 23:2). And so I began to distance myself from the grace of God.

But practicing spiritual disciplines to an excessive degree was not my only form of self-abasement. Although naturally I am fun-loving and excited about experiencing the wonders of life, one who loves to dream and look ahead to future events, I shaped a religious mask that included a pessimistic worldview I saw as biblical. I used preoccupation with the impending rise of the Antichrist and my own concept of the judgment seat of Christ as a form of self-flagellation. As I lost my ability to trust God about these things, I suppressed my natural excitement and jovial demeanor beneath a mask of somber intensity. I lost my sense of humor and particularly the ability to laugh at myself.

I felt afraid of lightening up, as though the weight of revival in the Body of Christ depended on my being able to focus on achieving it. God's wrath was something to be feared. He would not want me to enjoy the present too much, because I might begin to love the world and somehow become confused about His purpose in my life. Consecration, I believed, meant obsessing oneself in the spiritual realm. I interpreted the Scriptures by my own experience, thinking I was "setting my mind on things above" (see Colossians 3:2).

No wonder God sent Jesus into a society in which religion had taken on this same sickly pallor! One of the principal ways Jesus aggravated the Pharisees was humorously pointing out their religiosity and mocking their preoccupation with useless legalistic detail. His statement that the Pharisees "strain out a gnat and swallow a camel" (Matthew 23:24) was an absurd analogy that undoubtedly drew laughter. The Pharisees, who had carefully eliminated humor from their lives, were incensed. Jesus was too carnal, in their opinion, to be the Messiah they had waited for. Undoubtedly they expected the Messiah to be one of their own group—someone just like them.

In the same way, I expected that revival would come through people devoted to seeking it. I did not realize I had begun to admire ministries that were as infected with the leaven of the Pharisees as I was. Ministers whose newsletters attacked the church passionately for apathy and other sins of the flesh found my name on their mailing lists. I hung on their every word. I just knew there was no way these nationally known speakers could be out of keeping with God's Spirit. They had to be correct in their assessment of the lukewarm state of the Church. I was positive their condemnations of the fleshly indulgences of the Body of Christ were prophetic warnings to be heeded if we were to avoid God's wrath and experience revival. In these ministers I heard a confirming voice for my own judgmental attitudes toward others. Condemning others made me feel especially holy.

My teaching ministry was affected by the attitude I admired in other ministries. They confirmed my own opinions and strengthened me in my resolve to adopt the same approach. My messages during this period had an underlying "works" motivation. There were times, in order to prod the church to maturity, that I resorted to subtle threats of the loss of anointing or accused our parishioners of having a shaky relationship with God. Bill, a grace preacher himself, figured they must need my doses of intensity to balance the grace so they would not be apathetic. We did not realize that using shame and fear are the lowest forms of motivation and seldom, if ever, accomplish anything. Rather than inspire people to action, shame and fear discourage and suggest God is never pleased with their performance. Nor did I realize that any activity motivated by such messages will be wood, hay and stubble anyway because it will be done from obligation and fear, rather than from the pure joy of loving Jesus Christ.

How would someone who thinks he is serving Jesus Christ get sucked into this false spirituality? By refusing to look at the fruit. The Kingdom of God produces "righteousness and peace and joy in the Holy Spirit" (Romans 14:17).

When my brand of spirituality began leading me out of love and joy and into sins like pride and arrogance, I should have noticed. Instead of looking forward to walking with Jesus into the future, I began to feel anxiety about the future. As feelings of insignificance overwhelmed me, rather than resort to self-abasement, I should have admitted they existed and waited for the Lord to heal me. Instead of regarding others around me as apathetic to the cause of Christ, I should have enjoyed and loved them. And I should have realized that revival is a work of grace, an undeserved gift to the Church. Even the ability to pray for revival is a supernatural gift born of eagerness and spiritual hunger that we cannot contrive.

Steps to Healing

Thankfully the Lord did not leave me like a helpless sheep alone on a precipice. The church split caused me to feel the Lord's crook around my wayward neck. What a shock to look up and see that instead of following Jesus as I thought I had been, I had wandered away from the joy of His presence and was in danger of influencing other sheep in the same direction! God is always faithful to send correction in the most gracious ways.

Here is how I have been able to sort out what He did to bring me back.

Breaking Denial

In the same way that a drug addict needs to realize the extent of his or her problem, I needed to see that I needed help. My problem actually did resemble an addiction. It followed the same cycle as any addict who drinks, does drugs, gambles or shops compulsively. It began with the stress created in my life by low self-esteem and feelings of failure, since Bill and I had been unable to promote church growth. As my subconscious emotional pain increased, shame drove me to look for solutions.

Seeing the church grow was not my only motivation. I have always longed for the blessings of true revival. I wanted the joy of the Lord in my life more than anything. Seeking the blessing of revival seemed the most noble and selfless answer. But when revival is not in God's immediate plan and you do not know it, you can heap condemnation on yourself as you strain through obsessive praying and fasting to try to win this blessing.

This fruitless cycle caused me to feel stressed and resort to more panic-driven religious activity. It produced the same characteristics in me that an alcoholic demonstrates who is trying to attain and maintain sobriety: anger, impulsiveness, the tendency to affix blame, self-absorption, the need to control the environment, perfectionism, self-pity. I suppose you could identify me as a religious addict. Like any addict, I was in denial, until the incident with Dirk began to shatter my confidence in superspirituality as a means of getting God under my control. (God used other lessons in my life, too, which I will share later in the book.)

Introducing Nurturing Associations

During the next few years the Lord brought several relationships into my life that ministered healing balm to me. Bill and I became attached to the ministry fellowship pastored by the Rev. A. J. Rowden of Kansas City. His daughter, Roberta, and I became friends, and Pastor Rowden became like a father to Bill and me. Unlike the leaders I used to admire, he was full of love—a gentle, paternal spirit. I knew that his pastoral influence in our lives reflected the concern of the heavenly Father for us and our church. As we drank at the well of Pastor Rowden's church, associated with the other ministers attracted to that fellowship, and left the isolation of free-floating loneliness in the wider Body of Christ, I began to change.

We found not only the comfort of fellowship, but an influence that motivated by encouragement rather than authoritarian rigidity. Whenever Bill and I needed advice, Pastor Rowden (with great faith in God's ability to work things out) would not tell us what to do, but say simply, "Well, I remember when that happened to me. . ." and tell a faith-building story of the Lord's intervention in his circumstances.

The pastors in this ministry fellowship are usually not the headliners of Christian periodicals who compete for the pulpits of mega-churches, but men and women who find pleasure serving small flocks. Gradually through our association with these people, the Lord shifted our perspective of Him and His workings in the Church. I began to see the future as full of hope and the Lord Jesus Christ as full of love and grace and mercy.

We also learned much about pastoring that gave us confidence in our calling. Soaking in the Holy Spirit's ministry through Pastor Rowden's church and its ministry fellowship provided the encouragement and strength we needed to continue serving the Lord when we felt like giving up.

Bringing a Better Understanding of Grace

As we continue to fellowship with them and other members of the Body of Christ, I have noticed another healing change in my life. Participating in God-sent relationships can alter your perspective of who God is. Receiving what God wanted Bill and me to have through these relationships gradually drew my attention to His grace.

The Christian recovery movement, another healing influence in my life, revealed to me my need for more than a cursory look at the wounds of my past. Although the apostle Paul exhorts us to "[forget] those things which are behind and [reach] forward to those things which are ahead" (Philippians 3:13), I began to realize the Lord is also interested in restoring souls. The wounds of the past, as well as our failure to forgive the perpetrators and forget the things that have happened to us, are directly responsible for our inability to grasp the revelation of the grace that is in Christ Jesus. The Holy Spirit may give us gifts, callings and ministries, but without sufficient healing we will fall prey to snares such as the inability to trust God and to trust Him in others. These wounds and the scars they leave are like graveclothes that hamper our ability to love God and the brethren. They make it difficult for us to hold onto spiritual understanding.

In my early zeal to seek out deeper truth, I had begun to believe that my relationship with God was being jeopardized and that it was possible, if I did not keep "seeking God" with fervor, for me to lose any anointing I had, or even my salvation. Certainly I would not be able to experience the blessings of God, especially revival.

Now I began to see that my human frailties and the mistakes I had made in ministry needed the healing balm of

God's grace. One of the turning points regarding my ability to hear the Lord speak to me about my need for healing came through the book *Healing Grace: Freedom from the Performance Trap* by David Seamands (Victor Books, 1988). The revelation of God's grace in this book showed me my need and the difference between the false beliefs I was branding as spiritual and what was truly spiritual. Because of my tenacious belief in my own brand of spirituality, I had not always extended mercy to others.

Jesus loves the Church and does not condemn her, but seeks to bless and build her up. While Bill has always been a grace preacher and true pastor of the sheep, I needed to eliminate condemnation from my messages. And I determined never to use shame or the threat of lost blessing, regardless of the situation, to motivate the saints.

When I began to make a conscious attempt to speak edifying words, I noticed a change in my attitude toward the congregation, and a change in them as well. Rather than devote myself to obsessive fasting, I decided to love people. I further decided not to condemn them for their faults but give them space to grow, make mistakes, be imperfect and still keep my acceptance. If God would not motivate them through shame and fear, neither would I.

An interesting consequence of this approach has been that people in our church breathe more easily without having to live up to a minister's perfectionistic standards. They never did anyway. In fact, the church has come much closer to holiness and real spirituality since I gave the responsibility for conviction of sin back to the Holy Spirit. The members have the ability now to enjoy one another without having to act spiritual. Gone is the grave sobriety that used to characterize our prayer meetings. We are free to laugh and enjoy God and one another and pray at the same time. We are free to talk about natural things without having to punctuate every conversation with the latest heavy revelation we have found in the Word. This is because our acceptance of one another is not based on our ability to wear a spiritual mask. As the atmosphere has become more casual, the church has been freed from perfectionistic expectations and more open to the idea that God loves us already. We have stopped pressuring God to conform to our time schedule and have begun to attempt to flow with His.

Releasing Forgiveness and Expectations

Finding people to associate with who will allow you to be real is extremely important in the healing process. It is impossible to receive more than a small measure of healing as long as everyone around you expects you to talk spiritual talk and make spiritually "correct" responses in every situation. Look for friends who love the Lord and want to follow Him and who will also allow you to drop the mask and accept you, warts and all. In fact, in order to be healed, you may need to place some relationships on the periphery of your life, especially if they cause constant heartache and rob you of being able to feel God's unconditional love.

Now is a good time to ask the Lord to show you if you have caused hurt to others or have been unwilling to forgive anyone. If the Lord shows you someone you need to forgive, or someone you need to free from the bondage of your own expectations, do that releasing now. This will allow you to experience the same grace of God you may have withheld from those individuals.

As I have lifted the yoke of legalistic expectations I used to place on our congregation, I have begun to accept myself, mistakes and all, yet remain confident that God approves of me and will bring me into every good thing He has planned for my life. I no longer believe my salvation is in doubt. I know that what God has given me is permanent as well as precious. It does not require my own zeal and effort to either produce or protect. Jesus promised me, "I will never leave you nor forsake you" (Hebrews 13:5). Jesus Christ, the Good Shepherd, is the Author and Finisher of my faith. He is the guardian of my soul and is doing a wonderful job of it!

Now let's look further at the effect that the leaven of the Pharisees can have on a person's ability to develop relationships in a church.

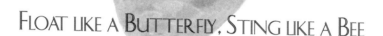

FLOAT LIKE A BUTTERFLY, STING LIKE A BEE

W hen Jack and Mavis become members of a congregation, they involve themselves in Meals on Wheels, outreach and prayer ministries. But intercessory prayer, they believe, is their real ministry, which is why they never stay very long in one place. In the fifteen years since they retired, Jack and Mavis have been members of at least eight churches.

When they joined the congregation of a minister friend of ours, they assessed the situation and found the church deficient in its prayer ministry. So this older couple began meeting with a few other members to pray on a weekly basis. But before long they left the church and moved on.

They do not cause division in a congregation but, without warning, hear from God that they are to leave. Their ministry done, they uproot and move to the next congregation to pray in a fresh moving of the Holy Spirit.

Jack and Mavis often refer in conversation to their devout prayer lives, their intimate relationship to the Lord and their ministry. They offer prayers in dramatic voices unlike the voices they use in normal conversation. In one meeting, while others were confessing their spiritual dryness and need for a new touch from God, Mavis blurted out that she had no idea people were in this state. "I always walk very close to the Lord," she added. This comment mildly wounded several in the room who had opened themselves up by confessing their lack.

Jack and Mavis left the last church after a particularly powerful worship service. Rather than enter the blessing of the service, they saw it as their cue to leave. Later Jack called the pastor to tell him that their work was accomplished, the Holy Spirit had moved according to their prayers and the Lord had instructed them to move on.

Examining the Fruit

Let's examine the fruit of Jack and Mavis' belief that God had spoken to them.

The Sting

When Mavis left the church suddenly, she left the Meals on Wheels and nursing home visitation committees without transportation two days before they had promised to deliver and visit. Jack, who had been assigned to find workers to cook and clean at the men's prayer breakfast that Saturday, left the group without anyone to cook. Apparently Jack and Mavis had little regard for the practical effects of their spiritual mandate. Perhaps they felt that practicalities should not be allowed to interfere with obedience to God, as though God does not understand the need to be practical. But if God is speaking to them, where are Christian love and concern?

As Jack and Mavis float from church to church, they do not realize they leave a sting behind. People who have come to count on them are left suddenly without a way to fulfill immediate responsibilities.

Lack of Accountability

Not only do Jack and Mavis' abrupt departures leave others holding the bag, but they raise another important question: To whom are Jack and Mavis accountable? They believe no other Christian has a right to question their communications from God and perceive such questioning as motivated by a controlling spirit.

But Jack and Mavis have a deeper problem.

Lack of Intimacy

They want desperately to minister but do not believe they need what other members of the Body of Christ have to give. Because they have difficulty developing interpersonal relationships, they have no truly close friends. Their religious masks are always in place as though they are afraid to let them down.

But a religious mask prevents vulnerability and self-disclosure, which are vital to developing friendships. By the time their newly acquired friendships advance to the level of heart-to-heart sharing, Jack and Mavis are out the door. They never question whether the Holy Spirit would ask an elderly couple to uproot themselves continually from a church just as they are making friends, only to place them in yet another unfamiliar situation. Jack and Mavis believe He would, because God's demands, in the face of eternal realities, are often exacting.

I wonder if Jack and Mavis do not realize, deep down, that their fear of intimacy makes them uncomfortable about self-disclosure in a relationship. They attribute this emotional discomfort to the Holy Spirit's leading them to leave a congregation. But without spiritual roots, their ministry is diminished. And their compulsivity prevents them from staying in one place long enough to have any lasting effect.

Jack is retired from a management position. He was practically a workaholic, devoting extra hours and time on weekends to the job. Now it is difficult for him to relate to anyone in a way other than manager to employee. Peer relationships are next to impossible. In fact, Jack and Mavis are not that close to one another. Their immersion in church activities gives them something to talk about without having to talk about issues between them. Without intending to, Jack and Mavis are becoming unstable souls, while they give the impression they know better than anyone what is truly spiritual.

And they have fallen prey to another unfortunate consequence of their belief that God has spoken to them.

Isolation

Isolation is the prelude to deception. If the devil can push us into a corner alone, away from the safety of the Body of Christ, he can cut us off from the protective influence of the Holy Spirit working through other Christians. I have never seen the devil show up in person. But he usually pops into our thought lives with spiritual-sounding suggestions or through someone who offers us some form of temptation. The Holy Spirit, by contrast, gives the ministry of pastoring, as well as the other gifts and ministries in the Church, to support and protect every member of the Body.

Outwardly Jack and Mavis give lipservice to their need for a church. But because inwardly they do not feel they need others, they are open prey for deception. Their thought lives, I suspect, are invaded with ideas that corroborate their desire to be in a class by themselves. Pride goes before destruction, but Jack and Mavis are probably not conscious of pride. Instead they see themselves as truly humble, putting their own needs aside and serving others in the Body of Christ.

Not paying attention to their own needs as individuals and as a couple has set them up for deception. The acknowledgment of need puts us into the category of humanity—a category the Pharisee wants to avoid. Being in this category means acknowledging weakness, which for the Pharisee is tantamount to failure. It means he or she failed to appropriate some spiritual gift or blessing that should have ministered to that need.

The failure to acknowledge need actually promotes the wearing of a mask and puts him into a category in which there are no peers who can treat him as he needs to be treated—as a normal human being. He wants to be separate, but what results is a counterfeit. In the interest of fulfilling scriptural admonitions not to love the world, this kind of pharisaical attitude gradually causes the believer to isolate himself from everyone, including godly influences.

There is yet another unfortunate consequence of Jack and Mavis' belief that God has spoken.

Superior Revelation

Victims of a pharisaical attitude can proceed into a realm of what they believe to be superior revelation. This can take the form of spiritualizing the Scriptures to exaggerate their meaning beyond what God intended. Since everyone interprets the Bible through the filter of his or her own understanding and experience, the isolated Christian can begin to believe that his interpretation of Scripture is divinely inspired, even if it leads him to damaging conclusions.

But beyond biblical interpretation, the isolated member of the Body of Christ can move on to the next step. Isolation taken to the extreme can produce delusional thinking, whereby an individual loses touch with reality. He can imagine that God is requiring him to do something from church-hopping to actually killing someone.

Law enforcement officials in the state of Israel report that each month at least two tourists become afflicted with what is now dubbed "the Jerusalem Syndrome." Individuals who lead normal lives until they come to Israel (according to an article in the April 17, 1995, issue of *Time* magazine) begin to hear voices and receive impressions leading them to believe they are incarnations of biblical characters, such as the two witnesses described in the book of Revelation who are to walk the streets of Jerusalem in the last days. These tourists do everything from disturbing the peace to perpetrating more serious crimes, believing they have a calling from God and are committed to function in a prophetic role. They are committed, all right—to psychiatric wards. Strangely enough, upon returning home they generally return to their normal lives.

Another extreme manifestation of "superior revelation" involves cult leaders like David Koresh, who believe their mandate from God requires them to develop a them-and-us mentality and resist the world. Koresh, having developed paranoid and grandiose delusions and barricaded himself in a compound with a small group of deceived followers, resisted governmental authority in the name of God while his obsession led men, women and children to their deaths. No one could penetrate his denial system because he had no peers. His followers were deceived by the belief that Koresh lived in an elusive, superspiritual realm that gave him divine authority to control their lives.

Jack and Mavis would never put themselves in the same chapter with David Koresh, of course, but they suffer nevertheless from a mild case of the same syndrome. I can identify. I know what it is like to live in a realm in which it is nearly impossible to receive correction. I felt secretly (although I concealed this from others) that there was no one as serious about God as I was to correct me.

When Jack and Mavis left their last church, Jack left the pastor no opening in the conversation to ask any questions. The pastor of the previous church, Jack told him, had suggested that going from church to church was not necessary for effective intercession. But Jack knew that in order to pray effectively, he and Mavis needed to be among the people to whom God was sending them.

The pastor realized the futility of trying to convince them otherwise.

Until Jack and Mavis drop their masks and entertain the possibility that they may not be hearing the voice of God, they will be condemned to church-hopping. Nor will their ability to influence the Body of Christ increase, because their reputation as church-hoppers will prevent them from being trusted by those who understand the importance of commitment.

Inability to Receive Ministry

Jack and Mavis rarely ask for prayer unless for some event, relative or person they have heard about. They never reveal personal need. The humility that enables a person to receive ministry is not yet part of their character.

"Freely you have received," Jesus told His disciples, "freely give" (Matthew 10:8). Receiving from the Lord through others is necessary for the development of Christian character, as well as for effective ministry. Before Jesus commissioned the Twelve as apostles, they were disciples or learners. In fact, it is important to remain teachable throughout life.

Paul, writing to the Corinthians, also indicated that every Christian is a member of the Body of Christ:

> For in fact the body is not one member but many.... But now indeed there are many members, yet one body. And the eye cannot say to the hand, "I have no need of you"; nor again the head to the feet, "I have no need of you." ... And if one member suf-

fers, all the members suffer with it; or if one member is honored, all the members rejoice with it.

1 Corinthians 12:14, 20–21, 26

Jesus Himself needed to be ministered to, receiving food, shelter and help from others. He took the time to train disciples and other co-workers in the ministry, implying that He believed He could not do the job alone. He even looked forward to the day when He could ascend and leave the work to His followers under the guidance and empowerment of the Holy Spirit.

If Jesus thought He needed others, why should we feel exempt? The truly spiritual Christian recognizes his or her need for the rest of the Body of Christ. It is not merely a mystical need, but a practical one.

The Pharisees of old, on the other hand, always took the role of instructor and even loved to be called "rabbi" or "teacher." In no situation did they reveal a need for ministry. To admit they needed anything would have required humility; and they were not about to validate Jesus' ministry by seeking His help. It was no coincidence that Nicodemus, a Pharisee, made his way to Jesus at night.

In the same way, Christians who never make themselves available to receive ministry refuse to validate the ministries of others. In the Pharisee's mind, no one is spiritual enough to impart anything to him. If ministry *from* others is optional, so is commitment *to* them.

Fear of Commitment

Jack's fear of commitment is one of the issues behind his inability to feel close to others. In fact, he was abandoned as a child—an experience that left him vulnerable to spiritualizing his problem. His fear of abandonment has left a gaping emotional wound that, because of his sophisticated appearance and spiritual mask, remains concealed and fester-ing. If others got to know him well enough, they might actually address this need, but opening up to others is something he secretly dreads. Rather than admit to God that he dreads it, he has convinced himself that he does not need to be committed to and faithful in a local church, as others need to be. Commitment to a body of believers would open him to the possibility of more rejection and represent another source of discomfort.

For Jack and Mavis to be committed would also link them with a peer group—tantamount to admitting they are like others in the group. So, in order to justify themselves and avoid feeling average, Jack and Mavis refuse to commit themselves.

But instead of allowing the Lord to help them understand why they feel uncomfortable with commitment, Jack and Mavis cover themselves with spiritual fig leaves, much as Adam and Eve did after the Fall.

The tendency to spiritualize away existing problems is a chief characteristic of a Pharisee. It prevents them from acknowledging sin and their need to receive ministry from others. This only perpetuates guilt and keeps freedom elusive by offering a religious cloak for shortcoming.

Commitment to a healthy local church in which they could learn to receive ministry as well as give it would help Jack and Mavis blossom. But their unwillingness to submit to authority for fear of losing the freedom to do as they please keeps them from it.

Jack and Mavis are not the only people with this problem. The larger Body of Christ has many disjointed members who have difficulty receiving and who cover this need with spiritual words and claims of divine revelation. The root problem: a form of self-centeredness that thrives on a sense of superiority and results in isolation that leads to deception.

How to Tell If God Is Directing

How can Jack and Mavis discern if God is telling them, time and again, to leave a church and move on?

Test God's Voice

Before the Lord expects us to obey a voice or impression, He wants us to determine if the voice or impression is His. Jesus said, "My sheep hear My voice, and I know them, and they follow Me" (John 10:27). God does not tell anyone to violate His character and divine nature through any guidance He gives. Jesus sent the Holy Spirit to build up the believer and the Church, and to create not disharmony but unity in the Body of Christ.

The principal question Jack and Mavis should ask themselves is this: Does the idea of changing churches every year hurt the Lord, others and ourselves? Jack and Mavis are blind to the hurt they are causing all three. In their zeal to obey God, they have left love, the most basic requirement of Christianity, in the dust.

What love is shown by leaving those who are counting on you in their hour of need? No doubt human ministries do come to an end, but the Lord will show you a gracious way out of a situation that will not leave others helpless. The Holy Spirit was sent as the Helper, and every word that is truly from Him will result in the ministering and receiving of comfort and help.

Test against God's Word

Another test is that of integrity. It is not necessary to pray about committing a sin that is clearly forbidden by Scripture. The Word of God reveals that disobedience to earthly authority is sin. God does not move in shady ways or use questionable methods. His ways are always free from sin.

One man driving down the road prayed that if the Lord wanted him to leave his wife for another woman, He should make every stoplight green. This way the man would know God was giving him the green light to commit immorality. But admonitions like "Thou shalt not commit adultery" (Exodus 20:14, KJV) were the only signs that man needed from heaven.

Nor did Jack and Mavis need to pray about keeping their promises. Fulfilling their commitments was the right thing to do.

And what about Jack and Mavis' special "ministry of intercessory prayer"? A special ministry of intercessory prayer is not one of the gifts or ministries mentioned in 1 Corinthians 12 or 14 or Romans 12. All believers have a ministry of intercession and are encouraged in Scripture to pray at all times in the Spirit and to put on the whole armor of God. Jack and Mavis feel that detachment from a local church is their cross to bear in order to be intercessors. But true intercession resembles the ministry of Jesus Christ, who according to the Scriptures is our Intercessor. His intercession involves commitment unto death; He gave His life in our place for sin. Preparatory to our own Christlike ministry of intercession, then, is having a community of believers we relate to and for whom we lay down our lives.

Various strange teachings about intercessory prayer imply that select Christians are called on to perform unusual acts of self-abasement in order to "stand in the gap" as Daniel did. Jack and Mavis feel called to a special ministry that relieves them of the need to submit to a local congregation and flow with the rest of the Body of Christ. Like the Pharisees, Jack and Mavis have begun to develop new regulations and standards for Christian discipleship based on twisted interpretations of the Scriptures that, as the apostle Peter warned, will lead to their own destruction.

Test the Fruit

Another test should be, Does the fruit of this impression lead me to love the Lord and His people more? Satan never directs you to love the Lord more, because then you might begin obeying the Lord and abandon the kingdom of darkness. Obeying the leading of Jesus, on the other hand (Jesus who is lovable and always loves unconditionally), causes us to love Him more.

The problem comes when we must be around those who are difficult to love and who may not readily love us. It is harder to feel close to the Lord when our involvement with others we do not love so well reminds us of a deeper need to grow. But John was right: ". . . He who does not love his brother whom he has seen, how can he love God whom he has not seen?" (1 John 4:20).

Isolated individuals like Jack and Mavis feel spiritual because they have chosen to avoid individuals who are difficult to love. They never have to learn to forgive because they do not linger around anyone who could offend them and so remind them that they are not behaving spiritually. The Holy Spirit, whose commission is to make us one that the world may know Jesus is real, does not lead believers into isolation, leaving them open prey to the subtle invasion of pride.

The church-hopper is usually a wounded person who has become secretly (if not overtly) cynical about the integrity of ministers or the capacity of other Christians to wound him or her. Unwilling to look at the lessons behind the wounds, the Christian caught up in modern-day Pharisaism does not believe that a church or pastor is truly conformed to his own standard of spirituality, whether it is extremely strict or radically free to oversee him. Rather than learn to trust Jesus about this, he is led by his fear of spiritual abuse to proud isolation.

If only Jack and Mavis could open their hearts to begin to test their impressions against the Scriptures and the God of the Scriptures! People like them are wounded souls who carry from place to place the weight of their unresolved emotional difficulties. Rather than seek a ministry to validate themselves, Jack and Mavis would be a more powerful threat to the kingdom of darkness if they allowed the Lord to remove their masks so they could be healed. Instead they justify their impulsiveness with spiritual words and miss one of the greatest joys of being a Christian—the close fellowship of the saints.

People like Jack and Mavis are not the only kind of Christian vulnerable to the leaven of the Pharisees. In the next chapter we will look at what happens when the leaven of the Pharisees spreads to leadership.

5

BOARD TO DEATH

Harold Sanders has served on the board of elders in his church for more than thirty years and is a well-known, financially prosperous member of his community. (His and other names have been changed but this story is true.) No one but church insiders, however, as well as a string of wounded pastors and their wives, have known until recently what Harold is capable of doing in the name of serving Jesus Christ. Harold's church has been unable, since the death of its founder, to keep a pastor any longer than three years. Once a particularly tenacious pastor held the job for five years, but he, too, finally gave up in dismay.

Harold is executive director of a large corporation that for decades has bought out every competitor. The success of his company has given him a reputation as a shrewd business-man, and he is often consulted by corporations that are struggling. But Harold's advice, though legal, has a ring of ruthlessness.

The church, recognizing Harold's success in the business world (as well as his generous tithing), has always elected him to the board. Many believe him to be a guardian who can see better than anyone how the church should spend its money and avoid financial disaster. They also trust him to confront the pastor when necessary, thus protecting the congregation from anyone in that office who may have ideas about leading the congregation in a direction it should not take. Harold enjoys the role of guardian and accepts his responsibility seriously, playing the devil's advocate whenever new ideas are presented in board meetings, especially by the pastor—whom Harold perceives as a threat to his position.

Several members of the church board owe Harold favors. His help always comes with a backslap and comment like "I know I can count on you when I need you." Nor does Harold flinch at calling in those favors when conflict arises in the church and he needs allies.

At one time Harold wanted to be a minister himself. His knowledge of the Bible is intimidating; he can cite chapter and verse for even the most obscure texts and he is sought out as a Bible teacher. Whenever he opposes any proposal, he speaks in pious tones of the Lord's will and cites Scriptures out of context to imply that God also disapproves.

Over years of serving on the board, Harold has been responsible for having pastors ousted for a wide range of perceived imperfections, from not punching a clock with a forty-hour week to having an unsophisticated wife. Each unsuspecting pastor is victimized because when Harold is on the pulpit committee, as he is every time, he comes across as spiritual, loving and supportive; but when he feels threatened by the new pastor's popularity, he launches his opposition. One pastor left after only two years when every one of his ideas, except the one to replace the copier, was systematically shot down. Harold took the bids on the copier and awarded the job to a salesman whose bid was not the lowest, since Harold wanted a discount for his own office.

The most recent conflict erupted when Pastor Lewis, after being at the church for eighteen months, wanted to begin holding renewal meetings on a night other than the ones on which services were already held. The purpose of the meetings: to bless members of other churches and attract the lost to Christ. Revival had begun to break out in a city nearby and it was spreading rapidly. Pastor Lewis, hungry for God, knew that the church had facilities large enough and could bless the community. Harold raised questions about the format, speakers and kinds of people who would be attending, then gave his reluctant approval.

Revival indeed broke out as a result of the new services. The meetings filled the church to capacity and went on week after week. It was not uncommon to see the conviction of the Holy Spirit come on even the most hardened. And the mayor of the town was converted to Christ.

Harold grew increasingly uncomfortable with the services, however, in which messages were preached by pastors in the community in addition to Pastor Lewis. One minister spoke on integrity and used an illustration that hit Harold close to home. In fact, it was so exact as to fit a situation at work in which Harold had been involved—an involvement that some Christians would have regarded as dishonest. Pastor Lewis noticed from a few rows back that Harold began to fidget nervously and glance around.

Many, meanwhile, poured down to the altar. Some sobbed while others were overcome with joy as they were touched by the Lord. Some stood up under the leading of the Holy Spirit and confessed faults. Harold appeared agitated but did not get out of his seat.

Later that evening he phoned several board members. The minister had spoken too long, he said. Those who had come to the altar had been too emotional. Visitors might be offended and not return to church. They did not want their church to become known as fanatical, did they?

All but one board member were surprised at these concerns. All felt intimidated. But knowing Harold's power, and that their positions on the church board could be at stake, most agreed to go along. A board meeting was called for Tuesday night to discuss the revival meetings.

That Tuesday evening Harold read several passages from the Bible about not creating division in the church and about not offending the weaker brother. Speaking with sincerity and emotion, he conveyed his deep concern that the Lord be glorified. Then he called for a vote to shut down the revival meetings at the church. Those who owed him favors voted with him. Pastor Lewis, who had been gratified by the fruit of the meetings, was stunned and grieved.

Harold may have feared that the pastor would find other ways of disturbing the status quo, so he went further. He set up a vote for Sunday night after church to keep or dismiss Pastor Lewis. In that denomination a pastor had to be retained by a congregational vote every year. If one-third of the membership voted to fire him, he would have to leave.

After the Tuesday night meeting, Harold launched a telephone campaign, inviting into the controversy everyone in town who had ever been on the church rolls.

That Sunday night the church was packed. In the pews sat dozens of concerned church members, most of whom loved Pastor Lewis and favored the revival meetings wholeheartedly. But more than a third of those attending had heard about the controversy through Harold—people who had not been to church since the new minister had arrived and who had not attended the revival meetings. When the vote came, Pastor Lewis stood twenty votes short of affirmation. He had to go.

Since that night several years ago, it has come to light that Harold was involved sexually with a woman who lived across the street from the church. Harold, although reprimanded by the board, was not asked to step down.

The revival meetings continued at another church in town and people kept getting saved. But since the dismissal of Pastor Lewis, it has been difficult for the church to find an experienced pastor. Word has gotten out in the denomination, as well as in the town, about the kind of church it has become. Attendance there has dropped. Those who do not want the church to stay under Harold's control have moved to other churches in town. But some adherents became so disgusted at the hypocrisy that they have not gone back to any church.

Pastor Lewis, realizing that he and his family could not endure the emotional trauma of a yearly popularity contest, left the denomination. He now pastors a loving church with another denominational affiliation. But he often reflects on what might have happened if revival had been allowed to continue. None of us will ever know.

Let's take a close look at what caused this ecclesiastical disaster and how it could have been prevented.

Woe #1: Wanting Respect

The scribes and Pharisees, Jesus said, "love the place of honor at banquets, and the chief seats in the synagogues, and respectful greetings in the market places, and being called by men, Rabbi" (Matthew 23:6–7, NASB).

When Harold was growing up, he feared his father, who was an abusive alcoholic. There were times Harold felt so angry and out of control that he would beat his pillow at night and swear one day to get even.

In spite of his shattered past, Harold accepted Christ at age twelve at the church his mother attended regularly. He gave much thought before graduating from high school to becoming a minister, and after graduation began seminary. But when finances were tight and he felt compelled to stay near home to protect his mother from his father's abuse, he left seminary and never returned. This filled him with further resentment. He often reflected on what his life would have been like had he been able to fulfill his ambition to be in the pulpit.

Harold's sad childhood conditioned him emotionally to fear situations he did not control. But because he is not conscious of this fear, he has sought religious cover for his wounds. Covering up the true problem has produced in Harold a powerful anger that manifests itself in control and manipulation. There are times when his inability to conform others to his wishes causes him to burn with anger, but his sophisticated mask conceals it, and he lets it out in a form of "punishment." He withdraws approval or robs others of their success by saying no—not after seeking the Lord's will honestly and developing an attitude of cooperation, but simply because he feels like it.

Some of us (more often than we want to admit) become frustrated at home or at work and let out our anger at church. Wanting to control *some* area of our lives, we make life miserable for fellow church members, especially those we may perceive as threats.

Harold's home is not happy. In fact, his wife does not sleep in the same bedroom and has her own pursuits. She resolved long ago to make a life for herself since Harold rarely includes her in his. This has caused him to feel out of control at home, and to both fear and hate what a woman can do to him. He transfers those feelings onto women in general and finds subtle ways of demeaning and excluding them from all church business except secretarial work.

Church is the one area of his life, even more than work, in which he feels in control. The people in his church make the mistake of assuming that Harold's business acumen is a spiritual gift. In fact, it is an acquired skill that has become perverted by the sin of greed and gets in the way of godly church management. Thinking he knows exactly how to administer anything, including a church, and perhaps believing that

God has given him this ability, Harold plunges ahead, cutting off ideas and promoting his own agenda.

The Pharisees of Jesus' day also perceived their role as guardians of the faith. They, too, were angry men who may have grown up under the strictest surveillance and discipline by their own fathers, who were probably Pharisees themselves. They had memorized large portions of Scripture by the time they were thirteen. Not only did they adhere to the written Law but to the oral law and traditions of the Pharisees, a body of thought based on the sect's interpretation of Jewish law. It was not uncommon to see a Pharisee on a street corner accompanied by a scribe carrying or rolling along a set of scrolls for immediate reference, lest any infraction go unaddressed. From the time they were children, the Pharisees had been scrutinized constantly and had learned the art of intimidating others under their control by using tradition and Scripture as offensive weapons.

Jesus did not fit their understanding of a Messiah—an understanding they believed to be based solely on Scripture. But beyond attempting to discredit Jesus, the Pharisees were threatened by His authority. They loved honor and being known as spiritual, and when their "spirituality" did not produce acts of power, and when the masses began to compare their speculative teaching to Jesus' ring of authority, the Pharisees deceived themselves into thinking He was a threat who needed to be eradicated.

A person who must control is deficient in his ability to trust God or trust others to God. He feels he must take responsibility for other people's lives and actions. He may feel relief at small victories when others conform to his wishes or standards, but this never satisfies him. He continually seeks more control.

The idea that only one person knows what is best for the congregation is a manifestation of pride. This person usurps authority from the pastor or leadership by holding up every proposal to his or her own standard of measure and rejecting it if it does not fit. Seldom does he get past his natural antipathy to change. Like every controlling person, he fears change and goes to great lengths to preserve the status quo.

Then there is the issue of respect. The perfectionist like Harold feels guilty for not being perfect. Guilt promotes his or her inability to feel love and derive satisfaction from pursuits. When these basic human needs are not met, he or she develops an insatiable desire for approval and being known as someone important. This leads to the sin of pride, causing the person to seek position rather than the responsibility of servanthood, the true path to leadership.

When pride motivates our striving for position, it is difficult for us to humble ourselves and admit our need.

Woe #2: Quenching the Holy Spirit

"Woe to you, scribes and Pharisees, hypocrites," Jesus said, "because you shut off the kingdom of heaven from men; for you do not enter in yourselves, nor do you allow those who are entering to go in" (Matthew 23:13, NASB).

The legalistic control of a strategically placed Pharisee can circumvent God's grace and thwart the work of the Lord. Harold's pride resulted in one of the most serious sins of Pharisaism: quenching the Holy Spirit—first in himself, then in others. Harold's anger developed into ruthless rigidity that ruled him without regard to its harmful effects on the church.

Harold may have looked uncomfortable during that service because the Holy Spirit was convicting him of sin. But if so, he toughened himself, rationalizing about the minister's preaching methods and what he deemed the overly emotional responses of others to the work of God. The result: Harold became an enemy—at least in this situation—to the cause of Christ. He did not allow the Lord to touch him and he prevented others from being touched, too. Pretending that he was acting in the best interests of the visitors and the church, Harold distanced himself from the conviction of the Holy Spirit.

The board meeting and congregational meeting were his grandstands. Harold loved inquisitions. He manipulated the crowd, especially those who had not been part of the revival meetings, describing the gatherings in the worst possible light, using words like *fanaticism* and *emotionalism* and quoting Scripture to elicit anger and fear. He led the people to believe Pastor Lewis was taking the church in a dangerous direction and acting out of impure motives. He even went so far as to suggest that the new pastor's collaboration with other churches in town was opening him to deception. He was not, Harold suggested, a pastor loyal enough to the denomination to lead one of its finest churches.

Harold had often brought up frightening tales of how pastors had fallen into immorality or made off with church funds. He always followed these statements with the sanctimonious phrase that "with God's grace it won't happen here." But the church that thought it was protected by a multiplicity of elders and immune to control by a pastor found itself manipulated by the very thing it feared—but in the person of an elder.

Ironically the church had taken pride in its form of government. This is nothing new; I have seen practically every form of church government work and every form of church government fail. The key is not usually the form of government but the character of those in leadership. Harold's church insulated itself not only against the possibility of an unscrupulous pastor but against the capable leadership of a genuinely godly one. Although God will always find a channel for His blessing, sometimes He has to flow around those who will not yield.

Woe #3: Religiosity + Anger = Hurting Others

What about Harold himself? The behavior of such people is often a cover for immorality. Perhaps his guilt over sexual lust and clandestine affairs was assuaged only when he was conducting a crusade that made him feel holy.

Harold's moral life is too close to the way Jesus described the Pharisees: whitewashed tombs "full of dead men's bones and all uncleanness" (Matthew 23:27). He was concerned more about how the church conducted business than about keeping his own life from immorality. Rather than admit his trouble and receive help, he allowed anger to feed his sin—which is why he created false crises and systematically took out every pastor who came along.

More about crusading and inquisitions later in the book, but I believe you are getting the message. Harold bears responsibility for untold emotional trauma in the pastors' families, to say nothing of the church people who have had to adjust constantly to new leadership. But it gets worse.

One pastor's wife had to be hospitalized for a nervous breakdown after her fragile emotions were crushed under Harold's heavy foot. She was the pastor's wife Harold felt was not sophisticated enough. She did not dress professionally or, as he put it, "know how to carry herself." She was no asset to her husband's ministry, he said, and certainly not the type to be "first lady" of his church.

Harold made life miserable for them, denying the pastor his annual raise and even refusing to spend money to fix the plumbing in the church-owned parsonage. But Harold did not wince when it came to tough decisions in business or in the church. God's work must go forward, he assured others on the board.

Could *I* Be Hurting Others?

Is it easier to see how the sect of the Pharisees could influence the crowd and the governing powers to have Jesus crucified? They whipped people into a frenzy with sanctimonious words and murdered without the slightest pang of conscience the Messiah for whom they had waited. Their lust for power and the anger that drove them to emotional numbness made them capable of murder.

In the same way, the person who is more concerned about acting spiritual than becoming a servant of Christ and the Church will eventually hurt the cause of Christ.

How do you know if that person is you? And what can you do to avoid it?

Step 1: Recognize Anger

Admitting anger, although we are sometimes afraid to do so, is a necessary part of opening the wounded heart to healing. Recognizing anger and seeing how you might be using it to hurt others around you is a step toward humility.

Have you ever felt like punishing anyone by withdrawing from them or by withholding something they want? Do you sometimes feel you need to show other adults around you who is in control by making them prove their loyalty with obedience? Do you feel numb emotionally? Do you make others conform to your "rules"?

These are some questions that help uncover a root of anger.

Step 2: Give Up the Need to Control

Until now you may have seen the need to control others as a good quality, perhaps even a mark of true leadership. But a person mature in his or her ability to trust God can also trust others to God without manipulating them or using force to make them cooperate. True leadership seeks to inspire to action rather than resort to the lowest forms of motivation, which are shame and fear. Manipulation always takes advantage of a person's negative emotions to produce the desired behavior.

Recognize that the need to control, and resorting to manipulation to accomplish it, are rooted in emotional difficulties from childhood. Perhaps the recent past will help you realize that these impulses need to go. Your security cannot come from your ability to control others, nor does God expect you to control anyone, except perhaps your own children. (After they are adults they, too, are responsible for their own actions.) The need to control, manage and manipulate to achieve goals is called codependency, an emotional dysfunction that may need to be addressed by professional counseling. But you can take a giant step toward healing by simply learning to let go.

Step 3: Let God Have Control

Harold needed desperately to let go of the church, but he was unable to do so because he believed he knew what was best in every situation. Others, he feared, would handle decisions unwisely or lead the church into a building program or other expensive undertaking that would demand sacrifices of time and money. A lover of tradition, Harold preferred to change nothing. The old ways, he was convinced, were better. After all, they had been good enough for the past.

Harold had not yet discovered the freedom of allowing others to bring in fresh, creative ideas and make decisions and take responsibility for their mistakes as a positive pathway to maturity. By making every decision himself and tabling other plans indefinitely so that "we can all pray about the Lord's will," he prevented the church from maturing.

Some church members wondered why no pastor wanted to stay very long, but no one knew for sure because board business was kept top secret, ostensibly "to prevent gossip."

Step 4: Get Out of God's Way

True humility makes us able to see when we become obstacles to God's best. Harold's pride had blinded him to the fact that he was responsible for cutting others off from the Kingdom of God. In place of discernment, he had substituted his fear of emotional displays—a fear he had cultivated throughout his childhood.

Although we will discuss this fear in depth in another chapter, let me give this warning. Substituting fear for discernment can happen to any of us before we know it when we speak against something we do not understand (as Harold did against the demonstrations of emotion in the revival meetings). It can also happen when we are too quick to examine our thoughts and motives thoroughly before we act. But isn't it better to err on the side of grace and freedom than on the side of law, where we are more likely to make God conform to our rules of church etiquette?

How many times did Jesus behave in a way that made the Pharisees uncomfortable? Discomfort should never cause us to negate another's experience with God. If it does, we can, like Saul of Tarsus, find ourselves fighting against God. After all, wasn't God's activity in the lives of the people at the altar of Harold's church worth the expense of a few sobs or even some joyful outbursts? I think Jesus would say yes.

What Can Be Done about Harold?

Perhaps Harold is someone you know. Harold needs love and grace if he is ever to repent, but he should not be allowed to continue in a position of authority—at least until he undergoes considerable healing. Perhaps, because of his adultery, he should not hold a position of authority because of the reproach it would bring on the church. Harold needs to surrender to the same discipline he metes out so quickly to others for less serious infractions.

What can be done to prevent his doing further damage? This depends on the form of government in your church and the amount of influence you have in Harold's life. Are you in a position of authority that gives you the right to speak to him? If not, does Harold have superiors in your church government? If you are not his superior in the denomination or ministry fellowship, and if you are not a person he respects, more than likely he will not listen to you. If this is the case, maybe all you can do is vote for someone other than Harold when it is time for board elections.

If you are a person with either authority or influence in his life, first be certain it is not you who are the Pharisee in the situation. You may be perceiving wrongly out of your own hurt and anger. Another person's offenses do not give you the right to behave out of anger and resentment toward him or her. Such action is not redemptive. But if Harold has a track record of incidents like the ones we have discussed, something must be done. How you do it is all-important.

Take it through proper channels. Jesus gave guidelines for discipline in Matthew 18. If neither Harold nor your church will listen, you have a choice to make. If you can bear the situation and trust God to move in your congregation, you may want to stay and pray. If you cannot endure with faith, you may have to do as others did in Harold's church and leave quietly and graciously. It is not worth the emotional expense, and your strength is better spent on the Lord's positive agenda. Sadly, He may already have given up, too.

People like Harold are not the only ways Pharisaism can attack the Church. Let's move on to another subtle form of it— a form that produces anxiety in the life of a sincere believer.

6

My Lucky Phylactery

(And Other Shortcuts to Spirituality)

Bill was leading Wednesday night prayer meeting at our church in inner-city Pittsburgh. As the group dismissed for fellowship, I overheard the hoarse voice of a middle-aged woman talking to my husband above the din.

"Reverend Fish," she began in a nasal tone, "will you pray over my lottery tickets and bless them for me? The Lord wants me to have a ministry and this is how He's going to provide."

Everything Baptist in me fainted. Not only is the lottery not the usual method God uses to launch a ministry, but can prayer and lottery tickets ever go together?

Even before I heard Bill begin gently to decline, I wondered at the woman's theology that provided for imparting a spiritual blessing on objects like lottery tickets while promoting a compulsive behavior like gambling and the longing to get something for nothing.

Why Search for Shortcuts?

This theology can entrap any sincere Christian who wants desperately to be spiritual or who gets in a bind. An emergency opportunity for ministry arises and God seems not to be within fifty miles. Nor is the preacher around to help, nor anyone else who may have remembered morning devotions or fasted last week. In that moment the earnest believer is left to face, with inadequate methods, the current crisis Satan has sent across the stage of life.

One recourse: to employ one of the many shortcuts made available by Christian authors like me who wrap up their books with neatly arranged formulas. It all seems so easy. Just use the method that worked for them and results will be forthcoming. The temptation is terribly pressing to find a quick fix for a dilemma—whether it is the need to discover the root behind Satan's latest trick or to say the right phrase in a prayer that will release the power of God.

Let's talk about just two situations that motivate the need to find a spiritual shortcut.

Pleasing or Appeasing?

Jesus was tempted by the devil, before He was released into ministry, to prove His identity as the Son of God by jumping off the Temple and trusting God to catch Him. Jesus did not succumb. But the woman anxious to prove her spirituality or power to minister can fall for this temptation. And the man who knows that without faith it is impossible to please God, but who is confused about what God is asking him to do, can end up not pleasing the God who loves and understands him, but appeasing the voice of the enemy in his own soul.

The temptation to "jump and let God catch you" challenges our idea of who God really is. If we see Him as perfectionistic and always setting the prize just beyond reach, we have an inaccurate impression that affects our behavior, mode of worship, interpersonal relationships and every way we try to serve God.

One of the greatest hurdles to Christian maturity is overcoming the emotional impulse to work for God's approval. Before we come to Christ, and sometimes for years or a lifetime afterward, we can remain stuck in this false impression. The greatest lesson of maturity is replacing this emotional impulse with the revelation of God's grace and love as what motivate Him to seek a relationship with us.

But as long as you think you want God and what He has to give *more* than He wants you and wants to bless you, you will stay on a treadmill of works, generating activity subconsciously to prove yourself to God, and prove to others that you really love Him and that He is honoring your efforts with demonstrations of love and power.

As long as you believe you want God more than He wants you, you will be afraid of losing your relationship with Him, His anointing and gifts and the best He has for your life. Instead of being a "led" person, you will be a driven person with a curious mixture of workaholism and Christianity—which lead only to anxiety and fear. At a subconscious level you want not to please but to appease God.

The sincere person who gets tired on this treadmill does one of two things. First, he or she may spend the rest of life in a state of hopelessness and rejection. Why? Because appeasing God truly *is* impossible (and unnecessary!). Or the person may simply give up and run away. People in this condition often leave the church and go back to their old lives. They believe they are rebelling against God, but they are really rebelling against their false views of God. They have yet to experience what it is like to walk with the God whose image is not the product of their own emotional needs. Following the true God for the right motives makes finding spiritual shortcuts unnecessary.

When we see God as unpleasant to get to know, we sub-consciously avoid Him and look for quick ways to obtain answers, shortcuts to spirituality. When we feel pressured by others to perform spiritually to their satisfaction, we opt for the quick fix. Perfectionistic and needy people always want something from us and are seldom satisfied with anything we do. They want a fast answer for their troubles. If Jesus were here in the flesh, they believe, He could relieve their misery in one instant—and they expect the same from us.

As Satan tempted Jesus to use the power of God, they will tempt you, too. Just learn to say no.

The sincere desire to please God is not the only reason people seek shortcuts to spirituality. Another is the desire to have a ministry.

Desire for a Ministry

Early in my spiritual career I learned from watching others in the Body of Christ that it is not O.K. simply to love the Lord and be a regular Christian. Regular Christians, I thought in those pre-scandal days, do not have power-packed ministries in their local churches and certainly do not find their faces on TV or in Christian bookstores. In order to "amount to a row of pins" (a Southern saying my parents always used to refer to a person not living up to his or her potential), you needed to have a ministry.

Ministries set people apart, give them an identity. Regular Christians look up to people in ministry. Their acts of power are legendary. Their pictures appear on fliers attached with magnets to the refrigerators of the Body of Christ. Regular Christians clamor for their tapes and feel awed to meet them. These are the spiritual elite we all know live in a higher realm and have escaped the corruption of the world, which includes anonymity and the need to eat, sleep and conceive children. At one point there seemed to be a stampede of ministry wannabes depositing their business cards throughout the Kingdom of God.

Mystified about the keys to their power to prevail with God, I pored over their books and tapes, looking for what amounted to shortcuts to power. How could I, too, dig breathtaking insights out of the Bible and pray for people and see God help them?

The search for shortcuts, often not on a conscious level, is usually motivated by a sincere desire to love and serve God but is born out of an insecure heart. Underneath my own spiritual search was not phoniness but an earnest desire to find out what made these ministry leaders tick. Why had God chosen them? I wanted to feel chosen myself.

Needing to be needed, seen or thought well of lies at the root of more ministries than we realize. Insatiable need sometimes "calls" a man or woman more loudly than the Holy Spirit. The person who thinks he is answering the call of God when he is merely filling an emotional need in his life may wake up one day disillusioned and feeling more like a failure than when he started, still conscious only that he wanted to serve God. Even those genuinely called by God can suffer from these emotional gullies, aching to be filled by the wrong things.

In New York's Kennedy Airport one day, I saw a battery-operated miniature of the Statue of Liberty. When the green rubber statuette was placed near a radio, it would sway back and forth as though dancing to the tunes coming across the airwaves. This, to me, is the picture of the Christian who needs to be needed. She is begging to help the "tired, the poor, the huddled masses yearning to breathe free"— whether by seeking approval from others, by trying to please a parent who never gave validation, by being diverted from the Lord's true call, perhaps by something else—but she is dancing to someone else's tune.

The need to be needed, besides yielding physical and emotional exhaustion, can lead to serious temptations like the desire to be competitive in spiritual things. Striving with others creates feelings of jealousy and the need to eliminate the competition. Put financial need in the pot and you have a recipe for something really ugly.

You may be driven not only by the wrong motivation for ministry, but by the right calling with the wrong means. Ministers who overspend and overextend can find themselves way out beyond the Lord's support and living in constant stress. In order to compensate, they grasp at quick fixes that make supporters believe more is being accomplished than really is.

This emotional baggage, unless removed, will inevitably lead to serious consequences, which often include moral failure and emotional burnout. Anyone placed in a position in which he has to "perform" constantly will discover a crying need to find shortcuts to powerful results.

Before Jesus began His ministry, He was tempted by Satan to gain world-renowned power and influence. Had He not already settled the underlying issues of the need to feel significant, He would have been vulnerable to use His ministry to meet this need.

Lucky Phylacteries

If you do not avoid the temptation to prove to yourself, God or others that you are spiritual, or the temptation to use ministry to meet personal emotional needs, you may begin to use spiritual activities almost as lucky charms. You would never put it in these terms, of course, but you get the sense sometimes that serving God is like rubbing a lamp and expecting a spiritual genie to jump out. You find yourself expecting answers to prayer, divine protection and power from God by doing the right things, in something akin to a form of divination.

The same belief system that makes a baseball player wear the same "lucky" socks for an entire season without washing them made the Pharisees put their confidence in a tradition that originated in the Law of Moses. Before the Israelites left the desert heat to enter the Promised Land, God commanded them through Moses to love Him with all their hearts, and to "bind [these words] as a sign" (Deuteronomy 6:8) on their foreheads and hands as a reminder of their own personal covenant with Him.

The Jews took God's command literally. By the first century B.C. they inaugurated the custom of wearing phylacteries—small boxes containing four important Scriptures and secured tightly to their foreheads and left hands with strips of leather. God had intended them to be simple reminders of Israel's relationship to Him until the Messiah came, but by Jesus' day they were worn as signs of piety to the outside world and used as good luck charms.

God promised the Jews originally that constant reminders of His love for them and their responsibility to respond would cause them to be blessed. But as their sense of closeness to Him faded, phylactery-wearing alone made them feel the security of God-promised blessing. When they needed a particular blessing, they paid careful attention to putting on the phylactery with precision. When any misfortune occurred, they saw as a possible cause the failure to wear the phylactery properly.

The Pharisees are not the only victims of such bondage. Even today, when we have the sense that God may be looking for a way out of His promises to bless or protect us, don't we tend to treat Him as the Pharisees did? We search for formulas, rituals and spiritual disciplines that we hope will ensure God's blessing.

I described in chapter 2 my extreme dependence on the rite of fasting as a way of showing God I meant business about wanting revival. Let's examine some of our other sacred cows.

The Bible

One of my most prized "lucky phylacteries" used to be the Bible itself. I don't know why I felt that God would not bless me unless I could find the proper verse or passage to support my need for a prayer to be answered, but I did.

As a young mother I used to pray, "Lord, I want You to save my children because Your Word says, 'Believe on the Lord Jesus Christ, and you will be saved, you and your household'" (Acts 16:31). Those last three words of the prayer I usually uttered with a louder voice.

If I had a sore throat, I felt compelled to find verses on healing and hold them up in God's face. Or if I needed a financial blessing, I reminded God that He had promised to supply all my needs.

My children broke me of this habit. When I had to postpone things I had promised them, they would whine, "But Mommy, you promised!" Children would make great attorneys—they are such legalists! My son and daughter must have scanned everything I ever mentioned as a possibility and demanded it at the moment they thought they should have it.

Well, when I asked the Lord for answers and followed my requests with chapter and verse Scripture references, as though I were talking to a law library in the sky, I began to hear the voices of my children. I could only imagine that God, who was my loving heavenly Father, might feel insulted at being treated like a distant relative! Then I read, "Your heavenly Father knows that you need all these things" (Matthew 6:32, NASB).

Devotional Times

Not only did I use the Bible almost as a charm, but my devotional time began to degenerate into a ritual.

In the church I attended as a child, we were required to mark our offering envelopes by checking off the following categories: *Attendance? On Time? Bible Brought? Daily Bible Reading? Offering? Lesson Prepared? Preaching Attended?* If we could check each box, we received a total grade of 100%. In order to be sure I could make the grade every Sunday, there were nights I would startle myself awake when my eyes were drooping shut. *Yipes! I forgot to read my Bible today!* I would sit up dutifully in bed, get my Bible off the shelf, read a verse—"Mahalalel lived sixty-five years, and begot Jared" (Genesis 5:15)—and slam it shut until tomorrow night.

Even after renewal came, I gradually developed disciplines at the advice of other Christians that I thought were more spiritual, including the need to develop a devotional hour. As time wore on, these devotional times became less pleasurable and more perfunctory. In fact, rather than praying during the day and carrying on a running conversation with the Lord, I found myself postponing the urge to pray until my devotional time the next morning. Gradually I started dividing my relationship with God into neat little parcels of controlled time. If I missed a devotional time, I began to feel God would not bless my life.

Tithing

It is important under the new covenant to give at least as much as those under the Law were commanded to give. Jesus Himself told the Pharisees to tithe but not to leave justice, mercy and truth out of the picture. But believing in tithing is different from being afraid not to tithe.

The hostess of a Christian television program in another state revealed that the previous week her husband had called long-distance to say their car had broken down. "Honey," she responded immediately, "did you put the tithe check into the offering last Sunday?" Until then she had not realized how she attached the threat of financial setback to their

tithing. In that area of her life she was living under the Law
and felt subject to its curse of retribution.

Ways to Avoid Being Cursed

This woman's fear underlies many of our other "lucky
phylacteries"—little rituals we perform to ward off evil from
our lives.

Many of God's promises in the Old Testament came with
legal contingencies, since Jesus had not yet died for sin and
since God was dealing with the human heart apart from the
Holy Spirit. He had to impose external constraint, for there
was no soft heart to be trusted to lead the godly through
questionable circumstances. Reading God's Law—which
compelled obedience—was the only way a person could
know what was godly in any circumstance and be protected
from evil. Everyone still lived under the curse of the Law.

The irony was, obedience was impossible to perform. The
Jews were supposed to realize this and be prepared to receive God's grace freely extended in the Person of the Lord
Jesus Christ. But they kept trying to be obedient to every detail of the Law and stayed on the works treadmill, dreading
the thought that they had somehow missed God and fighting a sense of impending doom.

The underlying motivation to ward off evil with some form
of appeasement is fear, which is part of every pagan religion.
Occultism is riddled with fear, as is any attempt at works.
When Christians miss the revelation of God as a loving heavenly Father eager to forgive and hungry for a relationship
with His creatures, we are gripped by fear of what might happen to us at His merciless hands. This fear makes us rely on
the fallacious cause-and-effect reasoning that underlies all
forms of superstition and causes us mistakenly to connect
misfortune in our lives with some sin of omission or commission. Some of the rituals we observe actually resemble

the proverbial holding up of a silver cross to ward off a vampire's attack. One Franciscan priest told an audience of Catholics and Protestants that wearing scapulars and putting the Virgin Mary on the dashboard will never replace the Fatherhood of God.

Every Christian denomination has its rituals. Most began as earnest attempts to preserve the faith, but sometimes we use them as substitutes for a relationship with Christ. The shadow becomes the center rather than the One who casts the shadow.

A teaching I heard attributed the misery experienced by the missionaries in a certain organization to the realization that the basement of its headquarters had not been purged of artifacts brought home by other missionaries from the field. These were thought to have made anyone who entered the building vulnerable to poverty and sickness—curses undoubtedly placed on the artifacts by sincere pagans.

After the artifacts were discovered and thrown out, one of the missionaries recovered from a serious illness. This healing was attributed not to the Lord's grace but to the discovery and removal of the pagan artifacts from the basement. Such reasoning (totally apart from the reality of demonic power) robs Jesus of glory for any act He performs. Instead, works-based human spirituality gets the glory.

Today in the same organization, frailties continue to plague the missionaries. To what cause should they attribute their current misfortunes? Are they to be sent on an exhaustive search for the cause of the supposed curse? How will they know if they have found the real root next time? Will they be sent back again when something else goes wrong?

Let's look at the ideas that "Someone may be praying against you" and that we should "Take care who lays hands on you for prayer." The thought that we should be hypervigilant about Satan's attacks throws many Christians into a panic, preventing them from resting in the protection of the Lord's will for their lives. Can't God sift through the negative prayers and decide not to answer them? Is He playing some kind of guessing game with you about where misfortune comes from? Will He leave you in a disastrous situation until you figure it out? Are misfortunes in life directly attributable to some chink in our spiritual armor, to an undiscovered spiritual threat, to our neglect to pay our tithe or pray diligently?

One Christian woman took up the habit of carrying a small vial of anointing oil in her purse. When she entered a Chinese restaurant, she would dab a little oil on her finger and anoint the placemats, lanterns and furniture to ward off evil spirits.

Let's examine the Word of God for precedents. As we look at the lives of Jesus and the apostles and their teachings in the New Testament, we do not find doctrines like these anywhere. Nor did Paul teach that we are to fear or be in awe of the devil. He did tell us we are dead and that our lives are hidden with Christ in God. There are consequences to sin, but these are obvious results of our own neglect.

Paul attributed his own trials to his mistakes or, more often, to Satan's desire to thwart the preaching of the Gospel. But even in his trials, Paul sounded like a winner and not a victim. "In all these things," he wrote, "we are more than conquerors through Him who loved us" (Romans 8:37). If the Lord Jesus Christ was on his side, he reasoned, then God the Father and the Holy Spirit, too, were in his corner. Paul even went so far as to say, "We know that there is no such thing as an idol in the world, and that there is no God but one" (1 Corinthians 8:4, NASB). He indicated that the fear of heathen idols was the sign of a new believer not yet mature in his confidence in God's ability to preserve him (versus 7–11).

Nor did Paul believe he was subject to the familial curses of his ancestors. He had made a decision to turn to Jesus Christ for salvation—he himself, apart from his forebears (see Ezekiel 18)—and was now righteous before God. Nowhere do we see Paul regularly rebuking demons off himself and other believers, fearful that unless he discovered which ones they were, they would be subject to their power.

He did not practice "pleading the blood of Jesus" over his car and wallet. He knew he was in Christ and that his life belonged to God forever. From the moment of his salvation experience, he was under the blood of Jesus and did not live his Christian life as though he were afraid of anything. He was not even afraid of the fact that once forty Jewish men bound themselves to an oath that they would not eat nor drink till they had killed him (see Acts 23:21). I guess the forty men are still fasting! Paul's wrestling with principalities and powers involved the power of simple prayers and big trust in a God who loved Paul enough to seek out his fellowship when he was lost and stumbling under the weight of acting spiritual.

Positive Confession

Early in my Christian walk, when I wanted to develop a faith that would be rewarded with power, I heard that you must confess positively. You would eat good or evil "by the fruit of [your] mouth" (Proverbs 13:2, KJV).

It is true that Christians look too often on the bleak side. But I went to the other extreme and became so bound by the fear of making a "negative confession" that I could not be honest about my feelings. I was afraid, for example, that simply by saying the word *flu*, I would contract it. Finally one day I realized that life had been simpler when I could just relax and have the flu. So I did. And the next time I got the flu, I used the time off to rest and read the Bible and Christian books that I had not had time to read. Now I get flu shots and my faith has grown anyway. My health is no longer based on my ability to confess, but on God's faithfulness.

While much of the Christian faith rests on the testimonies of believers, these testimonies should produce greater faith and trust in Jesus Christ to care for the believer. We have a right to reject anecdotal evidence that does not have a clear scriptural basis and that causes us to trust not Christ but our own ability to discover the root of evil, and fend it off by using some ritual.

So What Do We Do?

Are strange teachings keeping you from a sense of spiritual security? If it was more fun when you were unsaved, you know you are in trouble!

I encourage you to examine your faith for crazy doctrines that do not carry you through hard times without making you feel condemned or fearful. God is not spooky. Many teachings fall under the heading of *superior revelation* and contain an element of "secret" higher knowledge and a fear of retribution for those who are not privy to it. They exist with only the support of anecdotal evidence based on the cause-and-effect fallacy of reasoning.

What if good Christian practices like fasting and prayer or even taking Communion have degenerated into empty rituals? Do you fear that if you do not participate in them, you will be punished? It is time to learn that God did not invent these practices to make the Christian life difficult, but to make you more aware of His love for you. Jesus said to the Pharisees, "The Sabbath was made for man, and not man for the Sabbath" (Mark 2:27).

After the early days of my zeal, when I saw fasting as a way to manipulate God into answering me, I took a rest from it for several years. Now, only as the Lord permits and as I sense His blessing do I fast. Jesus' only requirement about fasting had nothing to do with length or even method—only that it be kept secret. One elderly minister advised me, "Fast only as long as it takes for God to have your full attention." This takes all the fun out of fasting for the one using it to develop his spiritual act. For him or her, fasting, praying and tithing all have a "must" quality to them, and from them the joy has long since ebbed away.

Talk to God often during the day. And for heaven's sake don't let the pastor starve or the church languish while you wait to feel good about giving! But why not reconsecrate everything you are doing to Jesus because you love Him?

Maybe the demon you need to cast out is the spirit of superstition. The Lord wants to free you from the fear of retribution, to live life without feeling like a failure and without looking over your shoulder for spiritually spooky causes for everything. He wants His sheep to lie down in green pastures; but sheep never lie down in the pasture unless they feel completely safe.

The more I have learned to trust God, the less I have needed my lucky phylacteries. His love is written on my heart. Now I have the substance who is Jesus Christ; I no longer need the shadow.

7

ABUSIVE BUT RELIGIOUS

Shelley met Bart at a prayer meeting just after she became a Christian. She had grown up in a small rural community in which everyone knew everyone else. Shelley had been an only child who socialized with the friends of her parents and had often felt the sting of loneliness. She had difficulty making friends in school. Looking forward to going off to college in a big city, she expected finally to break out of her mold and was determined to make friends.

Some of Shelley's new friends on campus were Christians who encouraged her to attend a prayer meeting of other students that met weekly in the off-campus apartment of two young men on fire for the Lord.

One of the young men, Bart, had grown up the child of a department store owner who was consumed with business and was seldom home. When he was home, Bart feared him because he often drank and became violent. Bart's mother cowered in the back room dreading the moment when his father got enough liquor in him.

The rest of the town had no idea what went on behind the heavily carved wooden and glass doors of their two-story Victorian home in the center of town. They did not know his father tormented his mother by holding a loaded gun to her head and slapping her mercilessly if she failed to perform every duty on the lengthy list he left for her every week. If Friday rolled around and the errands were not all accomplished, it was punishment time—Bart's father's night to drink and mete out the beatings.

The children did not escape. If grades were not in order or if toys were left on the porch during the dinner hour, Bart and his two sisters were beaten, too. Often they were told that they would never amount to anything and that they were a disgrace to the family name. Bart swore to himself that he would never treat his wife the way his father treated his mother.

The family had attended the Bible church three blocks away every Sunday for as long as Bart could remember. Each Sunday morning, weather permitting, the family walked to church in their Sunday best in front of home after home where no one was awake yet. Bart's father led the way, striding at least two or three steps in front of everyone and carrying a large Bible.

Bart found comfort at church listening to the Bible stories and sitting in the services. In this serene atmosphere he was free for a couple of hours from the threat of torment. Bart listened intently and began to see church as his place to shine. He became president of the youth group and was often called on to lead in prayer. On youth Sunday he preached the sermon he spent all year thinking about. He memorized long passages from the Bible and quoted them with sincerity, lending scriptural support to his views.

When Bart went off to college, he was relieved to take nothing of his home life with him except his faith—or so he thought. When he saw Shelley walk into the living room of his apartment, he set his eyes on her. Not long afterward they were dating regularly.

Bart was the first young man ever to pay much attention to Shelley, and she fell for him instantly. He always knew what to do in any situation and she looked up to him. It did not bother her that Bart had strong opinions about several things that she disagreed with, because he could usually support them with Scripture. She even overlooked the fact that Bart's temper sometimes got the best of him and came close to frightening her. She knew he was a fine person and just needed more love and attention, so she pushed these things out of her mind.

Bart and Shelley were married the first weekend after they graduated from college and moved back to Bart's hometown. Before long Bart's reputation in town grew as a man to respect. He was appointed president of the Junior Chamber of Commerce and an elder at church.

Bart and Shelley appeared to everyone else as if they were married happily and enjoying each other's company. But Shelley felt nervous about Bart's intimidating air and physical strength. He enjoyed roughhousing with her and pinning her to the floor. He would pull her arm up behind her back and hold it there for several minutes while he pushed her into a corner, then suddenly let her go.

One night when Shelley made an offhand comment, Bart grabbed her arm and began shoving her around the room. He raised his voice in a threatening manner, then seemed to realize what he was doing and released her. He sauntered off to his room and sulked for more than an hour. When he came out, he apologized and took her out for dinner.

All seemed better for several months. Then the company where Bart worked began to get into financial hardship. The pressure was on, so Bart escalated his performance and spent longer hours at the office to try to help the company navigate its way through stormy seas.

One night after he came home late, Shelley told him she had wondered how much longer he would be. Bart slapped her for the first time and shoved her onto the floor, calling her names. Again he apologized and promised never to do it again. But now Shelley was afraid that a force had been set into motion that could not easily be stopped.

Several years went by. Abuse turned into beatings. Shelley hated living in a small town where everyone worshiped Bart and she had no one to talk to. Once she hinted at her problem to the minister's wife, but the wife told her that she was sure the Lord would take care of it.

So Bart sings in the choir and teaches a men's Sunday school class. He often quotes Scripture to Shelley and reprimands her for her lack of zeal for the things of God. If she does not obey him instantly, he reminds her of her Christian duty. And as time passes the physical violence is increasing, while Shelley, afraid to expose the problem for fear of ruining her husband's reputation on which their lifestyle depends, keeps silent.

What's Wrong with This Picture?

The problem with this picture does not rest with only one person. Bart, Shelley and the church all play a role in allowing it to continue. Let's examine each one to learn how to recognize this form of Pharisaism.

But first, recall that Jesus rebuked the Pharisees more than once for looking beautiful on the outside but on the inside being like tombs full of unclean things. This is the leaven of hypocrisy. When a vocal public figure representing the Lord is exposed as not living the life he or she claims to live, it brings reproach on the Kingdom. Hypocrisy alone is probably the world's quickest defense against the Gospel of Christ. When the Holy Spirit convicts a nonbeliever, it is easy for him to point to dozens of people he knows who have claimed experiences with Christ, only to fall away or commit some deplorable act that shows God was unable to help them.

Christians use this argument, too, against the moving of the Holy Spirit. If revival comes and then a participant retreats to old patterns of behavior, the devil is quick to point out that the experience must not have been real.

But the Bible does not bear this out. In fact, such breaches of testimony were predicted by Jesus Himself, as well as by the apostles who wrote the New Testament. Jesus could do nothing with many of the people who followed Him initially for the excitement of the miracles He performed. Nor could He do anything with Judas Iscariot, one of His closest followers. The fact that Judas did not respond to help is no sign that Jesus was not the Son of God.

But there is always help for a person like Bart who is willing to admit the depth of his problem and seek help from the Lord and the Body of Christ. God can be glorified from situations like these if people like Bart and Shelley are willing to seek Him.

Bart knew he had a problem. He had survived a childhood of fear, a double life in which spirituality was integrated with abusive behavior and left to fester in secret. Bart's anger over having grown up a victim, helpless and out of control, had filled him with a cruel resolve never to get in that position again. Although he had sworn to himself that he would never treat his wife the way his father had treated his mother, he found himself acting out the behavior he had seen modeled before him every Friday night of his childhood.

So Bart determined to rise above the embarrassing situation, keep it concealed and try in other ways to compensate for his shameful secret. He chose the church as an arena for performance. Although Bart had truly accepted Christ and attempted to live by the Gospel, he could not get his anger under control. He was ashamed and remorseful about being a wife-beater, but had little access to help in a small town or the ability to remain anonymous in a support group setting. His shame, fear, anger and secrecy kept him on a whirling cycle of dangerous behavior that he could not control.

Shelley, too, had set herself up without realizing it for victimization. She had been brought up as an only child in a perfectionistic environment. She had been expected to behave like a miniature adult from the time she was a toddler, and had her own set of issues that made her ashamed to reveal any need for help. By the time she realized what Bart was like, she already loved him. Knowing nothing about the escalating patterns of abusive behavior, she kept expecting Bart to change, and for his remorse to lead to real repentance. It never happened.

The leadership of the church was unaware of the severity of the problem because of the cloak of secrecy that surrounded it. But had they known, it was likely they would not have known what to do. Their black-and-white, cut-and-dried approach to issues was fueled by a rigid approach to the Bible. This rigidity and the fear of suggesting disobedience to God's Word prevented them from looking at problems and seeing Christlike solutions. The letter of the law became more important than the Spirit, quenching the common sense that opened other areas of Scripture to their understanding. Afraid of allowing even the slightest variation from what they believed the Bible taught, they kept the entire situation in darkness.

Fear of relaxing restriction and thus giving over "holy ground" pervades the legalistic heart. But unless we understand the Pharisees' approach to Scripture, we will have no sympathy for those who hold these views, nor any knowledge of how to minister to them without attacking them. We will not see these attitudes creeping into our own spiritual lives, either.

The Pharisees and the Word of God

The ancient Pharisees were more like a fraternity than a sect of Judaism. Their beliefs, according to the standards of their faith, were orthodox, but the extremes to which they carried the observance of their faith set them apart.

The Pharisees did not even appear on the scene until a little more than 120 years before Jesus' birth, but they traced their roots back to the movement that restored Israel to the Scriptures after the Babylonian captivity during the days of Ezra, the scribe, and Nehemiah, the prophet-contractor who supervised the rebuilding of the walls of Jerusalem.

Proud of their heritage, the Pharisees were scholars of the Jewish Law who hoped to discover the mysteries of God and find a way of life that would ensure that God's favor remained on Israel. Failing to honor God and allowing His Law to fall into disregard had been responsible for Israel's seventy-year captivity in Babylon. It is not impossible to believe that the Pharisees saw the Roman occupation of Jesus' day as a sign that God's approval was about to be withdrawn and that judgment was imminent, perhaps even leading to another captivity in a foreign land.

So avoiding the disfavor of God became a life-consuming pursuit. It caused them to immerse themselves in several voluminous works, which are described in Alfred Edersheim's *Life and Times of Jesus the Messiah* (Eerdmans, 1977).

The first work—the one believed to be the most inspired— was the Halakoth of Moses from Sinai. These were the laws handed down by Moses and the patriarchs, along with logical conclusions drawn from them about the strict observances of their traditions.

In addition to this work was the oral law, another class of ordinances drawn up by the rabbis. Its purpose: to place a cushion of regulations around the Law of Moses. If a man obeyed the oral law, he was sure to find himself obedient to the heart of the Law, the Halakoth of Moses.

The oral law of the scribes or rabbis was another class of law open to discussion but one that carried the same authority as the others. These ordinances were discussed, voted on and imposed on a local congregation only if the majority agreed they could bear it. This body of law prompted Jesus to tell the disciples that the Pharisees "bind heavy burdens, hard to bear, and lay them on men's shoulders; but they themselves will not move them with one of their fingers" (Matthew 23:4). This curious aspect of the legalistic mind always imposes restriction or threatens punishment and offers no practical solution or way of escape. Jesus, on the other hand, came to lift the burden of the Law that men had for centuries been unable to bear.

Still another body of ordinances requiring strict adherence was found in the Mishnah, or the repeated Law. Another was the Midrash, divided into six orders of ordinances, subdivided into 525 chapters and 4,187 verses. It was a book of precepts, logically arranged, concerning contracts and law relating to daily life. Beyond these works were the two Talmuds or Gemaras—notes of the discussions of the rabbinical academies. They were full of theological anecdotes, law reports, legends, superstitions, even obscenities.

Imagine, then, the shock to the scribe who asked Jesus which of these laws was the greatest! When Jesus replied that loving God with all your heart, soul, mind and strength, and loving your neighbor as yourself, were the two commandments on which all the others rested, He pointed the way to a new fraternity of brothers and sisters who would have the purpose of God implanted supernaturally in their hearts so that even a child could tell what God wanted in any situation. But He was in effect making the Pharisees' chief pursuit futile.

Jesus taught that the Holy Spirit had inspired the Law, and that the strict observance of the letter of the Law killed while the Spirit gave life. In clarification, Jesus said repeatedly that He came to fulfill, not destroy, the core of the Law—the part of it that had been inspired by God.

Have you noticed that sincere, Bible-believing Christians—in the same way as the Pharisees—sometimes develop their own oral law or cushion around the Scriptures, full of do's and don'ts that are supposed to interpret God's will to everyone? In this way we have become guilty, like the Pharisees, of adding to God's Word by imposing on one another ordinances that are meant to ensure obedience but that wind up hurting each other and leave us no way out of terrible situations.

Some members of Shelley's church saw her submission to her husband as more important than her physical safety. They determined that preserving a marriage full of dangerous problems and keeping on a holy face for people around was what the Lord wanted in this situation. They decided for Shelley what would please God, based on what they believed certain Scriptures meant, while they neglected love, justice, mercy and truth. The motivation of love, which is the core of the Law, was lost.

Shelley, having been turned aside by the pastor's wife, was afraid ever to bring up the matter again. And Bart was afraid that revealing his problem would lead to negative consequences. He might never be able to live down his behavior or even remain in his hometown.

His fear of rejection by the church was real. He had seen others disfellowshiped who had sought help for problems and been unable to find relief in the time frame given by the church. Bart knew that if he could not conform, he would be unworthy of the church's love and robbed of its fellowship.

The church was imposing on Bart and Shelley an unwritten but firmly held code of spirituality to which they had to conform or be unworthy of their fellow members' love and acceptance.

Jesus attacked the Pharisees who questioned His willingness to violate their traditions in order to heal the suffering on the Sabbath. When He asked if any of them had been willing to save a son or even an ox that had fallen into a well on the Sabbath, they had no reply.

Sometimes we, too, like the Pharisees, would rather let a person suffer than help him out of his misery, if helping him is not spiritually correct. Before we know it, we can become

stern and rigid, black and white in our thinking. We withhold privileges and honor from others who muster the
courage to open their faults to the healing light of Jesus
Christ, rather than affirm them for their honesty. We can
even believe we are exemplary Christians because we have
such high standards.

What Should We Do?

In order to help a couple like Bart and Shelley, we need to
provide an atmosphere in the church that is merciful and gracious to the person who comes forward with a life-control-
ling problem. I am thankful for churches that allow those
whose lives have been scarred by addictions and other compulsive behaviors to step forward and receive more than a
quick-fix approach to healing. Bart and Shelley's church
needs to relax its tight reign of spiritual correctness that leaves
a person no room to fail. It is possible to do this while still
holding up the standard of a harmonious Christian marriage.

Providing counseling, support groups, even pointing
people like Bart and Shelley toward outside resources, would
lift the burden from their shoulders and do what the Body
of Christ is supposed to do: help us bear one another's burdens. Taking the time to show others how to have a happy
marriage and overcome the dysfunctions of the past is more
Christlike than merely preaching to them what they need to
do. Shelley knows she needs a home without violence. Bart
knows it, too. This is the desire of every couple that marries.

All too often, though, we emphasize what should be done
without showing people *how* to do it. It is not enough to admonish people to repent. Repentance means turning around
180 degrees. Convicting of sin is the Holy Spirit's job. Jesus
did not sit on His throne in heaven and shout through the
clouds all the things we were guilty of and needed to change.

Instead He stepped down off His throne, became like us, rolled up His sleeves and showed us how. But He did not stop there. He died on the cross, rose from the dead and sent the Holy Spirit to give us the same power He had. This is the Spirit behind the Law—truth mixed with luscious deposits of grace.

In the light of this Gospel, how should a church respond to people who are hurting?

Give the Freedom to Be Real

There are times in everyone's life when our pitiful experience does not match our glorious theology. We may be pointed toward the goal of holiness while living on its ragged edge. The church is to be a healing place where we can remove our spiritual masks and be ourselves. Masks only get in the way of God's work.

You can go a long way toward improving the atmosphere in your church by being real. Rid yourself of the need to conceal how you really feel, what you normally do or the problems you usually face. I am not advocating coarseness but gentle honesty. When someone approaches you with a problem, free him or her up by revealing a situation that helps you relate. Mutual sharing puts you on a peer level. Step down from your great white throne of judgment and identify.

Allow Christian friends to vent negative feelings about their situations without rebuking them. They know how they should feel, but perhaps they cannot feel that way right now. Let them know you have been angry about frustrating things in your life, too; that you accept them as they are and that the Lord loves them and will help them.

After you have given hurting friends your affirmation and the opportunity to express their pain, give them the grace or permission they need to grieve. Sometimes the solution to their problem involves a heavy loss, perhaps of a marriage or something they have always dreamed about. Think how you would feel if God were asking you for your Isaac. This will help you be compassionate and grace-filled rather than flippant and overly simplistic in your counsel. The Holy Spirit is known in the Bible as the Comforter. Let Him comfort others through you, and you will be surprised to see His supernatural grace and even His gifts flowing through you in a new dimension.

Help Others Get Assistance

Giving grace also involves knowing when to pass the problem on to a person who may be more qualified to assist. Do not overestimate your ability to help. Your friendship will remain constant, but a real friend knows that sometimes love alone is not enough, that professional help is needed. You cannot be the Messiah, but He will help you find relief for the hurting person. Encourage an addict to join a support group. Bart and Shelley need both professional marriage counseling and individual counseling if they are to overcome their problems.

A church should have a plan of action in place for a woman who reveals physical abuse in her marriage. The action plan includes a safe place of escape and long-term commitment to her to help her through her problem. Someone needs to guide her to the right social agencies so that she can survive financially while counseling is taking place. Many Christians now see that sending a woman back into an atmosphere of spousal violence is not acceptable counsel. Violence always escalates and often the husband, angry that she has revealed the problem, beats her severely. Do not think Paul was talking to women in this situation when he admonished them to submit to their husbands. Statistics about Christian women victims of domestic violence would make you shudder. The heavenly Father who loves us and

has our best interests at heart does not ask women to submit to violence in the hopes of saving their husbands. Jesus
has paid the price for everyone's salvation already.

Encourage Honest Accountability

Bart cannot continue in leadership in an unstable emotional condition that is likely to bring reproach on his church.
Removing the pressure of leadership is the kindest thing to
do, for many reasons. It is too difficult for a person to try to
be healed for the sake of the church. Better to seek healing
for oneself and learn to be content to love God for the right
reasons, rather than for the sake of external pressures. Even
though a leadership role may be down the road, making
someone feel the need to conceal his problem puts far too
much pressure on him now. This interrupts the next element
of the restoration process: accountability.

Sometimes in our zeal to see miraculous answers to
prayer, we think the battle is won when we have won only a
skirmish. It may be years before all the hurts in Bart's and
Shelley's lives—hurts that have contributed to the development of their tragic situation—are healed. They will have
testimonies along the way of God's grace. Let them give
them—but allow them to be realistic in their estimates of
what has really taken place. They may be so eager to please
and perform for the church that they submerge other difficulties and ignore their need to stay open to help. They must
remain accountable to leaders in their church as well as to
their counselors.

But those stewards of their accountability cannot afford
to be rigid and legalistic in their approach to help. You and
I are not giving over scriptural holy ground by allowing Bart
and Shelley to reveal a gap between where they are today
and where they want to be with God in the future. We did
not die for any scriptural truth. We can do nothing to make

people respond to God who do not want to; it is not our responsibility to hover over them and make them comply with our wishes. Some deposit of the Holy Spirit must be within them giving them the desire to change. Relax your legalistic expectations and surround them with love and acceptance as they let God change them.

What If They Don't Change?

Again, this is not our responsibility. Too often the legalist has an overdeveloped need to protect the faith and adhere strictly to the ordinances he has developed, which amount to his own oral law. We think we are cushioning others from a fall by imposing our restrictions on them. We are not. Sometimes shielding them from the consequences of their own choices makes them dependent on us to tell them how to act and what to do. We will be no more successful than the Pharisees of old who had to manage everyone's lives. No, each person needs to learn to respond to the Law written on the heart, and be given the opportunity to do so.

Bart and Shelley are separated. Both are receiving counseling now and the church is supporting them. Bart attends a mission church on the other side of town, respecting Shelley's fragile emotions. His presence would intimidate her and he knows it. This is a sign of repentance on his part. He can see the gravity of the problem his violence has created, and recognizes that it will take time and a lot of mercy from God and Shelley if their marriage is ever healed. Bart must accept the fact that Shelley may never again be able to trust him enough to live under the same roof. The church needs to help him through this time, too.

Trust and love are not the same. The story of David's pursuit by King Saul, his predecessor, is a case in point. Although David loved Saul and honored him, Saul was full of malevolence toward David. Saul so vacillated in his treatment of him that David knew Saul could not be trusted, even though he continued to love and honor him.

I hope that, with counseling, the story will end differently for Bart. And even though Bart needed to step down from leadership, can you imagine what kind of example he will become—if he receives help and overcomes his tendency to be abusive—of the power of God and the healing grace of the Lord Jesus Christ?

The church should maintain its commitment to Bart and Shelley as long as both are willing to walk with Jesus Christ in integrity. After all, Jesus promised each one of us that He will never leave us or forsake us. Isn't it time we lived that out, too?

8

WHAT SIN MADE THIS HAPPEN?

I was preparing spaghetti for dinner when the phone rang that Friday afternoon in October 1972. I heard the anxious voice of my mother on the other end: "Melinda, you'd better come quickly. Your daddy's in the hospital. He's had a heart attack."

My father had suffered heart disease for decades, but he was only 58 years old. As Bill and I made the six-hour drive to Houston from Fort Worth, where Bill was attending seminary, I had time to collect my thoughts and pray. A year had passed since Sarah Phillips told me about Pat Boone speaking in tongues. I had been touched by the power of the Holy Spirit, then become desperate (as I described in chapter 1) to find the secret to real spirituality. At the point that my mother called, I was in pursuit of miracle-working faith. Perhaps the Lord had brought me to a new understanding of His miraculous power just in time to enable me to pray for my father's healing. Hope began to rise in me that something wonderful was about to happen. Bill and I held hands and prayed that the Lord would move in my father's body and heal him.

As we arrived and stood at Pop's bedside, we saw him hooked up to a heart monitor and oxygen tubes. He was barely conscious. Hospital personnel were bustling about and monitoring the jagged line on the screen. Pop stirred and acknowledged our presence.

"I love you," he whispered.

Hugging him, I told him we were going to pray for him and ask the Lord to heal him. He nodded weakly, unable to speak.

By the next morning I knew we had stepped into a war for Pop's life. The faces of the doctors and nurses were somber. As the family gathered in the tiny waiting room marked *Chapel,* I knew this was no time to give in to fear and negativity. Throughout the morning we prayed and paced the floor as Pop lay in his hospital room gasping for life. Because I wanted to maintain confidence in the power of God, I resisted attempts to talk of anything except his healing.

We weathered several crises that morning. The nurses would pop their heads in the door of the chapel and update us on his condition.

At one point early in the afternoon, they asked one of us to stand by his side and hold his hand, urging him to breathe in the oxygen he needed to survive.

Praying that God would give me strength to do it, I took Pop's hand and leaned over him: "Pop, breathe!" The sound of my voice roused him and he inhaled. For a few seconds, at least, the heart monitor recorded a stronger beat.

We were going to win the battle; I just knew it.

At the end of the day, Pop was beginning to stabilize. God was honoring our prayers and my faith was beginning to build. I was thankful and encouraged.

I searched the Scriptures diligently and trusted verses of healing as specific promises to our family, Gibraltars under my feet. God's Word was sure. I also felt that God spoke personal assurances to me that Pop would be all right.

As the days wore on, he improved and Bill and I returned to seminary life in Fort Worth. For the next several weekends we made the long trip to Angleton, praying for Pop's recovery and looking forward to the day of his dismissal.

By Thanksgiving he was beginning to progress rapidly. Relieved, I accompanied Mother and Danna Kay, my sister, to Houston that Friday for a day of much-deserved rest while Bill stayed with Pop. That night we visited Pop and laughed together. When I hugged and kissed him as I left, I did not know it would be the last time.

Before we could get dressed the next morning, the phone rang. My mother bolted out of the house for the hospital less than five minutes away. A few minutes later she called. Pop had collapsed of another heart attack in the shower and died before he hit the floor.

The next few days were a blur. I clutched my Bible, which had been the mainstay in my life through the last few months; but grief was strong and had come so suddenly that I found myself fluctuating between periods of trust and bewilderment. I wanted desperately not to cry. Crying, I had learned recently, was a sign of unbelief. But before the weekend was over, I was wondering how I could make it through the next few months. And before the week was out, I wondered how Pop's death fit into my faith at all.

A Time to Question

Everything I had begun to believe during the past few months about healing and God's response to a believer's faith was called into question. I had been taught much about the rewards of faith. For several weeks prior to Pop's heart attack, I had sat in the meetings of one of the best-known faith teachers in the Body of Christ. According to his teachings, faith is always rewarded and doubt is always unrewarded. Miracles are simply a matter of exercising faith. Jesus was able to work miracles because He believed and did not question. He acted on His faith and saw answers. If only I could emulate His pattern and trust my heavenly Father, who wanted all good things for me, I would receive my heart's desire.

Well, if there had ever been a desire in my heart, it was for Pop to be healed. So in the weeks after his death, I began to examine myself to find the reason he had died. Why had I lost the battle for his life? Could I have prevented his death if I had tried harder to believe? If only I had known that my faith had not been strong enough, I could have adjusted my behavior to fit the challenge. What had I done wrong?

As the days wore on, my depression became deeper. I functioned in my job as a teacher's aide, fixed dinner and made it through to weekends, when Bill and I drove to visit Mother in Angleton. It was hardest there. Everything reminded me that Pop was never coming home.

My mother and sister, though grief-stricken, seemed to handle their pain better than I. Pop's death, though it had been a terrible surprise to them, too, had not cast them into a crisis of faith as it had me. Their theology at that point did not allow for a regular occurrence of miracles in the first place, so they processed Pop's death as the natural outcome of decades of heart disease.

At night I would awaken and remember that Pop was dead. Through tears I would run through the events of October and November, trying again to find the missing point of faith. I began to feel resentment toward God for not helping my unbelief. I would fight these thoughts, but many questions filled my heart. I tried to maintain a good confession of faith, a spiritual "stiff upper lip," straining to keep my trust in God. But how, I wondered, could I believe any impression in my heart again? How could I ever trust God again to heal anyone or answer any prayer I prayed?

A Vulnerable Faith

I did not know then that my belief system at the time of Pop's death, like other areas of my life, had become infected with the leaven of the Pharisees. In my impulse to purge my life of old ideas about the Lord—ideas that left no room for the miraculous—I had embraced the idea that God would respond to my faith today. The Christian book market in the early '70s was deluged with books about the powerful invasion of the Holy Spirit in the lives of ordinary people who had been spiritually destitute. Each book I read chronicled one miracle after another, leaving the impression that these lives were never mixed with the pain of unanswered prayer. Authors who did touch the subject left a more than subtle impression that for every unanswered prayer, there had to be a discernible cause. If it could be discovered and rectified, the answer would come.

Nearly 25 years later the Body of Christ has matured through suffering; Christian stores are stocked with shelf after shelf of books that offer answers to those left hurting when faith goes seemingly unrewarded. In an effort to respond to the groundswell of unexplained personal pain, we have sometimes leaned so far in that direction that we have lost sight of God's power in the present. Could this be what Satan calculated would happen by riding our zeal into a theological box canyon with no way out?

Unexplained suffering is one of the great mysteries of Christianity and a predominant theme of world literature. But in our feeble attempts to explain God's ways, we have created a theology that leaves no room for mystery. Unfortunately, many sincere Christians have been left devastated by a legalistic theology concerning faith and suffering—a theology so rigid that it leaves no room for any conclusion other than human failure to believe God adequately.

How is this possible?

Legalism and Suffering

Finding the answers to suffering is a strong theme in Jewish literature and the Law. The Pharisees taught that specific sins were met by God with specific punishments. A close look at the Law of Moses reveals many incidents in which God punished bad behavior with suffering. The flood of Noah followed centuries of disobedience, cleansing God's creation of moral decadence that had been perfected almost to an art. The plagues of Egypt that set the Israelites free from slavery visited unthinkable sufferings on God's enemies as a direct consequence of their rebellion. Pagan nations were punished by God for their idolatry through the armies of Judah and Israel, victorious because of their obedience to God. Even King David was subjected to evil consequences as a result of his sins of adultery and murder.

More than a little scriptural evidence exists for the belief that suffering is a direct result of sin, and that even the godly are not exempt. The Law of Moses became a taskmaster, wrote Paul, to open our hearts to our own sinfulness and its subsequent punishment. Under the Law, earthly suffering foreshadowed eternal punishment for those who did not have a good relationship with the God of Israel.

Law demands adherence. And when disobedience occurs, punishment must be meted out without respect to social standing or even relationship to the judge. The Law itself foreshadows hell. Oliver Wendell Holmes, Jr., an associate justice of the Supreme Court, wrote, "In hell there will be nothing but law, and due process will be meticulously observed." Living under the Law is hellish for anyone, especially the Christian who rejects being liberated from it and prefers its rigidity over learning to receive and give undeserved mercy.

In fact, the obsession of a perfectionistic individual with Scripture leads to deception. Paul, himself a Pharisee, wrote,

"The letter kills, but the Spirit gives life" (2 Corinthians 3:6). Looking at the Word of God without understanding His mercy will lead you to conclude that because your sin warrants punishment, your heartaches—and the misfortunes of others—are directly attributable to specific acts of disobedience.

Why would a Christian who has been forgiven of his or her sins embrace these beliefs?

The answer lies in our emotions. Because we are born with a sinful nature, whenever we commit sin (or even think we do), our internal condemnation buzzer goes off, reminding us that we need punishment now. When Adam and Eve sinned, no one had to tell them that they needed fig leaves and that they should hide from God. They did so out of the impulses of fallen human nature. They were compelled to hide because they felt ashamed of the sin they had committed. They were afraid of God and what He might do. They made up for their lack of glory with a pitiful natural substitute—fig leaves sewn together to cover their nakedness.

Under the Law, the best you can do is sin and dive for cover. You are trapped in a nature prone to sin and bound to commit something worthy of death. The only recourse is to minimize the number of sins you commit. This is the doctrine of perfectionism—the religion of the world.

Perfectionism demands a lifelong attempt to purge oneself of sin, to slow down the committing of it and rid oneself through any means necessary of its resultant guilt. Appeasing God's wrath by performance becomes the motivation behind every religious observance or spiritual discipline. "The gods are mad, bring out another sacrifice!" becomes the subconscious watchword of the zealous Muslim, Hindu, Jew, animist—and the legalistic Christian. Attempts to please God and earn His approval often lurk beneath sincere attempts to love, show kindness and good works. And when others do not meet our standards, we withhold grace and mercy from them because they failed to earn it from us.

The answer to this dilemma: Receive God's free gift of salvation in Jesus Christ, who died on the cross to save you from your sin. His blood alone can atone for any sin you have ever committed or will commit. Yielding to Him and hiding your life in His frees you from having to appease God by your performance.

When we receive Jesus Christ into our lives, we usually experience a great sense of relief as the burden of earning God's approval is lifted from our spirits. But it may take years before the impulse to appease God is erased from our emotions. In fact, the emotional scars of living under the Law may take a lifetime to heal.

My own tendency to seek God's approval and feel I had earned it made rigid teachings appealing to me. I thought I could control what God would do in any situation by holding Him to any scriptural promise I selected to fit any need that arose. Without realizing it, I had been led by my zeal into a rigid, legalistic approach to the Bible that clouded my view of God. Unless I could control God's actions in my life, I was afraid of Him. Not being able to control God meant I might fall prey to the temporal consequences of the sin of Adam—consequences like disease, death and the mistakes of others. Clinging to a legalistic view of Scripture provided a sense of peace. Life became explainable; every experience fit into a category. Good was rewarded with blessing, evil with suffering.

I explained the sufferings of others by reminding myself that they must have done something wrong or omitted something good. Perhaps they had not studied God's Word enough to dig out the insights that would have saved the circumstances for them. Maybe they had not prayed and fasted enough for Satan to loosen his grip on their situation. If they were ill, it was probably because they had not obeyed God and disciplined their bodies; maybe they had backslidden into substances like saturated fat and cholesterol.

Before my father died, I took refuge in the idea that if anything evil befell me, I would with God's help be able to find the root of the problem and make the appropriate behavioral adjustment to achieve the place of blessing. Because I was filled with judgment, I lacked the ability to receive and give mercy. Nor had I sat at Jesus' feet to learn His views on the subject.

Jesus' View of Suffering

One day the disciples asked Jesus about a blind man they passed on their way out of the Temple. Jesus had just riled the Pharisees by telling them, "Before Abraham was born, I am" (John 8:58, NASB)—a direct reference to Himself as the Son of God, the Messiah. When the disciples saw the man who had been born blind, they seized the opportunity to query the One who had the answers:

> "Rabbi, who sinned, this man or his parents, that he should be born blind?"
>
> Jesus answered, "It was neither that this man sinned, nor his parents; but it was in order that the works of God might be displayed in him."
>
> John 9:2–3, NASB

Then Jesus illustrated His teaching by healing the blind man.

The disciples' question reflected the common belief held by the Jews and taught by the Pharisees that handicaps, illnesses, accidents and other misfortunes were due to sin on the part of the victim, or someone who cared about him or her, or a forebear (based in part on Exodus 34:6–7). Affliction had been visited on the person as a form of discipline for not adhering to the Law.

This belief also undergirded the responses of Job's friends who visited him after everything he had was taken away.

They sat with him awhile, then began to offer suggestions as to why the terrible events had occurred that had cost him his health, his possessions and the lives of all his children.

In the book of Ruth, Naomi believed that the loss of her husband and two sons, as well as her subsequent poverty, had been caused by their leaving Bethlehem and living in the heathen land of Moab, a place God had cursed.

Zacharias and Elizabeth, the parents of John the Baptist, who had been barren until their old age, were thought to have been cursed by God and prevented from having children because of something they had done. Elizabeth believed God brought about John's birth to vindicate her.

So Jesus' teaching that the man's blindness was not caused by his sin or the sin of his parents represented a radical departure from the legalistic views of the day.

Another time Jesus was asked about the deaths of those killed by Pilate whose blood mingled with their sacrifices in the Temple. They were no worse than anyone else, He replied, nor were the eighteen people killed when the tower in Siloam collapsed (see Luke 13:1–5). Everyone dies and suffers misfortune because of Adam's sin. While we are still subject to the curses of physical infirmity and death, we will be liberated eternally through Jesus' death and resurrection. In the meantime, although we suffer, there are times when God enters our lives in supernatural ways to remove sickness and misfortune and even rescue us from premature death. It is Jesus Christ who should receive the glory for these events, not our own "superior" ability to have faith.

Jesus' primary goal, I believe, is not to prove Himself through miracles, but to alleviate the suffering of mankind. Signs and wonders reveal God's loving nature and confirm to us prophetically that there will be a day when God wipes all our tears away. But the Holy Spirit's workings are subject (as when Jesus walked the earth) to the will of the Father, who holds each person's life in His hand.

Does anything we do cause evil to befall us?

I don't know what God wanted me to learn from this. So I guess it came again...

There are deadly wages of sin. It is possible to shatter a marriage irreparably through adultery. It is possible to make unhealthful choices and diminish the quality of your life. It is possible to commit sins that result in accidents or even the deaths of innocent victims. It is possible to kill yourself. These and many more are the consequences of living in a human body subject to decay, and living alongside others who are also fallen.

The apostle Peter warned that when we suffer, we need to be certain we are suffering with a clear conscience. "If anyone suffers as a Christian," he wrote, "let him not be ashamed, but let him glorify God in this matter" (1 Peter 4:16). Let a Christian suffer, in other words, for the sake of the Gospel of Christ and not for crimes he has committed or as a result of sins like gossip, rebellion and spitefulness toward others. The principle of sowing and reaping, after all, can apply to sin as well as to the good seeds of the Gospel.

Identifying these causes of suffering is different from trying to find the obscure cause of a negative event you will never truthfully be able to discern.

And what if you do find yourself suffering directly for a mistake you have made? Because you are willing to give grace to others, you may expect mercy from God even if you do not deserve it. When you free others from indebtedness to your expectations, you open your heart to receive mercy from God. It is not beyond God to redeem even the worst mistakes and bring you to a place of peace.

It is at this point that you begin to understand the wisdom of God in your suffering.

What Good Is My Suffering?

I have long been assured that my father's death was in God's plan for his life on this earth. He had committed himself to the Lord. The number of his days were ordained for him (as the psalmist wrote in Psalm 139:16) from his mother's womb. If I can see no other reason for Pop's death, I can trust the character of my heavenly Father. God did not take his life away in order to teach me lessons. He would not regard my life's lessons above the well-being of another of His children. To think this would be proud, placing myself at the center of the universe.

Walking through this experience, part of the painful terrain of human experience, gave me several important positive realizations.

God Is the Center

Before Pop died, I did not realize I was developing a theology in which I was at the center and in control of my life, rather than the Lord Jesus Christ. In an effort to learn to walk in faith, I had begun telling the Lord what to do. Rather than ask Him how to pray, I assumed that my own spiritual experience and knowledge provided all I needed to know about the will of God in each situation.

Without intending to do so, I assumed that God's will was already revealed in the Scripture verses that were illuminated to me. I did not realize there was much of the Bible I had yet to understand, and probably never would in a lifetime. We cannot live long enough to fathom all the ways of an eternal God.

I learned to relax and let God run the lives of others as He sees fit. I learned to submit to the Lordship of Jesus Christ and accept His judgment in matters beyond my wisdom and control. A deep peace comes when you realize you do not have to figure everything out in order to be spiritual. In fact, it is a mark of true spirituality to trust without understanding God's reasons. All we need to know is that, regardless of how life turns out, "All things work together for good to those who love God . . ." (Romans 8:28).

2 *Let the Spirit Interpret the Word*

Not only did I not comprehend all the Scriptures, but I did not understand the Spirit behind the letter.

The Holy Spirit must be allowed to interpret the written Word of God to us in each situation. The written Word *(logos)* reveals the Lord Jesus Christ, the personal *Logos.* God's written Word builds a foundation of faith that teaches us what God is capable of doing. It also builds our confidence in His nature as we see how He has worked in the lives of others who have responded to His love.

When a person relies only on the written Word to determine God's will in a situation, he often mistakes natural denial for faith. When Pop was sick, I repressed any sense that I did not have God's mind and mistook this for faith. Continually I had to suppress feelings of uneasiness and began to imagine that God had given me Scriptures to hold onto. I was denying reality. Unlike Abraham—who believed God while realizing that his wife's body was well past the age of childbearing—I refused to look at the natural situation at all. After the initial crisis, Pop was still not recovering after nearly two months in the hospital. I was not humble before the magnitude of the circumstances. The denial that is the initial phase of grief had already set in, but I was unwilling and unable to recognize it. I thought I had a word from God.

The word of God that produces faith you can count on in a time of crisis is another Greek word, *rhema.* When Paul wrote, "Faith comes by hearing, and hearing by the word of God" (Romans 10:17), he meant the *rhema* or God-breathed inspirational word for the moment that reveals which Scriptures can be applied to a particular situation. Sometimes we must pray according to what we believe God's will is, because we do not always know His will. In those times we must leave God space to reveal His mind to us. He can help us learn to trust Him regardless of the outcome.

Scriptures cannot be applied indiscriminately to every situation—for instance, to an individual's need for salvation. It is not God's will that any person should be lost but that all should repent (see 2 Peter 3:9). But that is no reason to believe every person will ultimately be saved. Isolating one Bible verse or passage without allowing the rest of the Bible to interpret itself results, in this case, in the false doctrine of universalism. Jesus taught clearly that although hell was created originally for Satan and his angels, men and women who will not respond to salvation and will go there forever.

In the same way, verses about healing cannot be applied indiscriminately to every person's sicknesses and infirmities. Not every illness will be healed. Unless we are the last generation before Jesus Christ returns, an accident, infirmity or sickness will eventually claim each of us until death, the last enemy, is removed from the earth.

Don't Judge Others' Suffering

Another lesson I learned was to refrain from judging the sufferings of others. When I finally calmed down and called a truce with God, I began to learn how legalistic I had been in my approach to suffering. As I looked into the mirror of my experience, I began to see things about myself that were not Christlike, not least of which was my failure to love mercy.

I remember Pop, one leg swung over the arm of his rocking chair, quoting one of his favorite verses: "He has shown you, O man, what is good; and what does the Lord require of you but to do justly, to love mercy, and to walk humbly with your God?" (Micah 6:8).

When I looked in the mirror, I saw a woman who needed mercy, who wanted to be accepted and respected. But this woman was not willing to admit she did not understand why others suffered. She was proud of her ability to discern, quick to assign motives to others and relegate them to the back seat of God's bus. When others failed to be healed or obtain answers to prayer, I regarded them as lacking in their faith. The crisis of faith over Pop's death provided a schoolroom like no other to begin learning how to stop judging others.

It is none of my business why anyone suffers. My business is to show God's love and mercy, standing with that person and validating him or her through suffering. This is what Jesus did and more. He left His throne in heaven not only to learn what it was to suffer, but to suffer to the point of death on our behalf.

Allow Others to Grieve

Another lesson I learned was to allow others to grieve their losses and even express the same anger I had felt toward God and my circumstances. God does not need me to defend Him in order to maintain His relationships. Nor do I need to remind others who suffer of their need to trust God. I can stand with them, feel what they feel and understand that it takes the rich soil of valley experiences to grow a harvest of mountaintop faith.

Pop's death taught me that grief will not separate me from the love of God. Although I was severely tempted to run away from God when I discovered I could not figure Him out or control Him, I chose not to. My ability to choose this path was a gift from God. Without this gift I would have run.

Walking with Jesus through Suffering

I have learned that there are enemies of faith that cannot be met wielding the sword of the Spirit, the Word of God, with human strength. God does not release power that lets us function apart from a close relationship with Him. There are no formulas to obtain God's blessing that substitute for a close walk with Jesus Christ.

The Lord used this period of suffering in my life to begin unwrapping the graveclothes of a pharisaical approach to the Scriptures, which I was misusing and substituting for the true knowledge of God's voice in my life.

But this period of suffering did not negate my belief in God's power at work today. Since then I have watched many Christians who have been privileged to experience the healing power of God in their bodies. I have been healed myself and have experienced the welcome intrusion of a *rhema* of faith in several trying instances. Faith, I have learned, is not a matter of keeping up a good face in the midst of trial, but the gift of the Holy Spirit for unusual circumstances.

It is not necessary to act "spiritual" in order to obtain it, as though it were the product of human effort. Rather, it is the fruit produced by the presence of the Holy Spirit in our lives and a lifetime of learning to walk with Jesus.

9

WHEN PHARISEES GO TO THE MARKETPLACE

("My House Is Worth $20,000 More Because God Told Me So!")

R ay Smith, an experienced realtor in a nationally fran-
chised office, had put in weeks of work on a transaction
that would benefit both buyer and seller—the kind of deal
he enjoyed bringing together. The house was being sold by
Helen Collins, an elderly widow who needed to sell quickly
in order to move to a retirement village in another state. She
was overjoyed when Ray found Joanna, a middle-aged
woman with a good job who was ready, willing and able to
buy the property.

Joanna had testified at her church before house-hunting
that she was trusting the Lord to help her find the right property. She had lived in her current home fifteen years, had
saved enough money to buy another, larger home and was

excited to find Ray, a kind realtor with a good reputation, to help her in her search. Joanna prayed that God would lead her to the house He wanted her to buy. When she saw Helen's house, she fell in love with it immediately.

The house was located near Joanna's job and had all the amenities she had asked the Lord to help her find. It was even the right color—pale yellow with black shutters. It had been kept up and improved to the point that Helen could have sold it for several thousand dollars more. But because Helen liked Joanna and wanted to help her (even though Helen did not happen to be a Christian), she agreed to a lower price.

As Joanna prayed with Ray while standing on the property, she became even more excited. Then she went to Ray's office and signed the sales agreement without reservation, promising to buy the property as soon as her mortgage loan was approved. Ray changed the market information about Helen's house in the multilist computer to read *Under Agreement*. This removed the house from the active market to ensure that other buyers would not be shown the property before the closing.

Six weeks went by. The housing inspections were done, the loan applied for and secured and everything was in place for the closing. The closing attorney made several contacts with Helen and Joanna to make sure the closing went smoothly and quickly. Joanna seemed committed to making good on her signed agreement to buy. Helen was relieved that her name came up on the waiting list of the retirement village. Her apartment there was ready and she could move in anytime. If she could not move in a one-month availability window, however, her apartment in the village would go to the next person on the waiting list.

The day of the closing arrived. Joanna and Helen were to sign the final papers and Joanna would take possession of Helen's house. Movers were waiting to move Helen's boxes out of the house she had lived in for fifteen years and transport them to the retirement home.

After they sat down at the table to sign the papers, Joanna cleared her throat and announced that she had something to say. The night before, she revealed, she had had a dream. God was warning her that for some unknown reason she was not to buy this house. She had begun feeling troubled about committing herself to purchasing Helen's house and knew God was giving her misgivings to prevent her from suffering unknown negative consequences.

Everyone at the table sat in stunned silence. Joanna picked up her purse, took out her keys and left without another word. Setting her face to do the will of God, she left her dream house behind to obey God. Or so she thought.

A Word from God?

The weeks that followed were filled with heartache for Helen. The apartment in the retirement village went to the next person on the waiting list. She lost her deposit with the movers, who had canceled the move. Although she kept the deposit that had accompanied the signed contract, it was not enough to cover her costs and fees, because she had not asked Joanna for much, trusting her to come up with the balance at closing. Helen did not sue Joanna as the sales agreement permitted because she did not want to treat others like that.

Helen's house took another several months to sell. During that time she suffered a stroke, leaving her unable to move to the retirement village since she was no longer ambulatory. She had to hire extra help because her daughter, who had arranged for her to live in the retirement village, was unable to look after her. She had to move instead to a nursing home. Even though Helen recovered the use of one leg, she remained in unhappy surroundings unable to find a retirement home that would take her. She died earlier than she should have. According to her doctor, her depression over the circumstances broke her trust in people and contributed to her early death.

Ray, the realtor, had been counting on the money from the closing to pay part of his daughter's college tuition. He had sold several other properties recently, but they were in lower-priced neighborhoods and had brought minimal commissions. Ray was known for helping needy persons through the real estate process. He had hoped that the sale of Helen's house (she had been a friend of his mother's) would bring a better commission, for which he had worked long hours, showing the property to many potential buyers. As a result of Joanna's sudden decision to walk out of the closing, Ray's daughter had to work two jobs to make up for the loss and actually had to delay entering college for a semester.

The couple who finally bought Helen's house love it and are living in it happily today. Helen gave them the same price she would have given Joanna, because by that time she was desperate to sell.

Joanna cares little for Helen's misfortune. She still thinks she heard from God, even though she did not find another house as good as Helen's. In fact, the one she bought—the one she thought God told her to buy—was thirty minutes farther from her job and turned out to have a leaky basement.

I wish this story were fiction, but it is not. In fact, I work in the real estate office where it happened. (I have changed a few details to protect identities.) Believe it or not, Christians have a reputation in the workplace for doing impulsive things. More than one realtor is afraid to work with "born-again types" because they have a reputation for giving their word and then breaking it, citing as a reason that "God told me." Other Christians make unfairly low offers on properties, claiming divine revelation as their source of guidance, as though the Lord wants to cheat the seller out of a reasonable price. Rather than follow through on promises on which others depend, superspiritual Christians have done much harm to people like Helen, attributing it to Jesus Christ.

Pharisees in the Workplace

Jesus is opposed to this kind of behavior. It brings reproach on the Gospel and sometimes even keeps people like Helen out of the Kingdom. They are convinced that Jesus Christ is not real or that if He is, He cannot be trusted.

Jesus told those religious leaders, "Woe to you, scribes and Pharisees, hypocrites! For you devour widows' houses, and for a pretense make long prayers . . ." (Matthew 23:14). Joanna did not exactly devour Helen's house, but she definitely consumed her chances at the retirement village. Joanna's impulsive act crushed Helen's trust in people and even her desire to live. Joanna made God look foolish and put a stumbling block in front of an unbeliever.

Many Christians who want to be obedient can find themselves being Pharisees. Why do they act like this when they appear sincere in wanting to do God's will?

Joanna suffers from a distorted view of God that makes her certain God asks her to do unexpected, difficult things to prove her devotion to Him. Like many Christians, Joanna hears the voice of God through a wounded soul. Let's examine her background for clues.

Joanna's rigidity—which causes her to grasp for unreasonable solutions to problems without considering alternatives—has roots in a home where she had no father and a mother who was very strict. Joanna grew up being abused verbally if she spilled her juice or scratched her bicycle. This conditioned her emotionally to avoid mistakes at all costs and pursue perfection, because mistakes were always punished.

The church Joanna attended reinforced this emotional response and made a fetish of missing the will of God. According to them, not to pray hard enough or make the necessary concessions meant missing the "good and acceptable and perfect will of God" (Romans 12:2), and thus getting God's second- or third- or fourth-best for your life.

So Joanna was conditioned emotionally to hear God through a filter of perfectionism. She was afraid to make a mistake. When it came to decision-making, she always prayed first, but as God led her to solutions that seemed to hold the desires of her heart, she had second thoughts. Before reneging on her agreement to buy Helen's house, Joanna broke engagements to two young men. When the wedding dates drew near, she developed cold feet. Sometimes she heard a voice speaking to her in her thoughts, quoting Scriptures that began with the word *beware*. As time wore on, she became more rigid in her thinking and more wary of making major decisions in her life. In fact, she became paralyzed with indecisiveness.

Rather than consider the possibility that she has a problem, Joanna covers her fear of making mistakes with religious fig leaves. She calls it the fear of the Lord. Her emotions tell her that the fear of the Lord is the same as the fear of making a decision without God's express permission. In this way she pushes her indecisiveness off on God. God, in her view, never allows her to enjoy life or obtain anything she desires. Her own desires, she believes, must be inherently evil and "of the flesh."

Someone has said rightly that hurt people hurt people. So it is with Joanna. She is aching to find the God who loves her unconditionally, but she lives as though His love and approval depend on her ability to discover His will in each decision and live it out. If she does not, she believes she will suffer the consequences.

Her rigid attitudes make her unmerciful to others. Because she believes God is strict with His children to save them from the evils of this world, she winds up hearing unreasonable requests out of her own soul that masquerade as God's voice. She makes no room for trial and error. Taking the wrong path would, she believes, lead her out of God's protection. So she makes impulsive decisions without regard to how these decisions affect the lives of others. She is more concerned about being correct than about whether the results of any decision are full of mercy and good fruit.

But good fruit and the exhortations of Scripture are all-important when we are determining whether a certain course is the will of God. Joanna's so-called leading from God, rather than being authored by a God of love, was engineered by Satan, whose purpose is to kill, steal and destroy. All three of these rotten fruit eventually came out of her decision, but Joanna's religious pride keeps her from seeing and admitting it.

Let's examine what course Joanna could have taken that would have resulted in better fruit.

What Might Have Been

Joanna needs to judge her impressions by God's Word and the fruit of the Holy Spirit. And she needs to show unbelievers with whom she has dealings—unbelievers in the real estate office, for example—that hers is a God of wisdom and love. If Joanna had checked her decision against a simple litmus test—"Whatever you want men to do to you, do also to them" (Matthew 7:12)—she would never have taken the course she did.

There are at least four more criteria by which to judge an apparent leading of the Lord.

Consider Your Emotions

When Joanna had the dream the night before the closing, the first thing she should have done was consider her emotional reaction. Rather than produce peace in her heart, the dream made her feel disappointed. But because Joanna always feels that God wants to punish her wayward behavior, she is not wise to this tactic of the devil. She considers disappointment a clue that she is being asked to suffer for the cause of Christ, giving up her own desires.

Joanna also reacted to the dream with fear. She was afraid of hurting others and causing a scene at the closing, perhaps even incurring a lawsuit; but she believed God's will demanded strict, obedient responses, whether or not the world understood. Despite momentary compassion for Helen, Joanna concluded that if she gave into those feelings, she would be led to buy the house out of sentimentality for others. This would place her in opposition to the "good and acceptable and perfect will of God."

Beneath Joanna's emotions of disappointment and fear lay a sense of relief that came from not having to make a commitment. The fear of commitment causes many people to freeze and turn from a decision. Recall Joanna's unwillingness to follow through with either of her engagements to marry.

Every realtor is aware that many buyers experience jitters in the weeks before the deal closes. They toss and turn, have nightmares and wish they had never signed the papers. Some even keep shopping, thinking they are buying the wrong house and that another one would suit their needs better. But usually they come to recognize that this anxiety is rooted in the fear of making a commitment. Joanna, however, saw it as a sign from God.

Will This Action Bless Others?

In addition to examining her emotions, Joanna needed to anticipate the effect her decision would have on others. It is important that decisions reflect fairness and create a win-win scenario for all parties involved.

I am convinced that if a business deal is godly, everyone in the transaction will come out feeling blessed. For God to enable you to purchase a property at very low cost when it is worth much more would create a winning situation for

you but a losing situation for the seller. Although fair nego-
tiation is part of good business, too many Christians think
God will work miracles for them at the expense of fairness
to others. I have seen Christians resort to manipulative techniques and even lies to obtain the bargains they are looking
for. This behavior more closely resembles witchcraft—the
attempt to manipulate people and circumstances supernaturally for one's own gain.

When Joanna told everyone at the closing of her sudden
decision not to buy, the time for praying about the will of
God was long since past. She should have prayed longer before she signed the agreement to purchase. If she was still
unsure about certain elements of the deal, she should have
included contingencies in the contract that would have to
be met before she would sign the final papers. She did not,
so everyone took her at her word and proceeded with the
changes that would take place in their own lives after the
sale—changes that later were thrown into turmoil.

Joanna should have honored her word—if for no other
reason than Jesus' instruction "Let your 'Yes' be 'Yes,' and
your 'No,' 'No'" (Matthew 5:37)—and kept her part of the
bargain. Instead, she actually lied by signing a sales agreement and failing to honor it, and in so doing ended up hurting others.

Is It God's Wisdom?

Believers must also make certain that anything they attribute to God's will is wise. Joanna's assertion that God did
not want her to buy the house after all made Him look
dumber than the average realtor! She not only broke her
word, but made a poor decision by giving up Helen's property in order to purchase an inferior house later on at a higher
price. Had she proceeded to buy Helen's house, she could
have signed the papers, relisted the house with Ray and sold

it herself at a profit within a short time. But Joanna failed to buy the house God had led her to and wound up purchasing a property unsuitable for her, because she allowed unreliable emotional responses, rather than godly judgment, to govern her decision-making.

Joanna's mistake would not fall under the category of Pharisaism except for the fact that she attributed all this bad fruit to God. When a Christian makes a mistake and realizes it, he or she should have the humility to turn around and go the other way. If others have been hurt, he or she should apologize and seek to rectify the mistake, even making restitution when appropriate.

What Effect Will It Have on Unbelievers?

Joanna was not about to make restitution to Helen—which would have cost her money—when she would not even admit wrongdoing. But this made onlookers think that Christians are concerned only with making a buck at someone else's expense. When Joanna walked into the closing unsure of herself, she should have known that keeping her promise was the loving thing to do and that God would help her even if she had made a mistake. But covering her fears with a religious mask made the situation odious to the unbelievers involved. I heard the Jewish broker at the real estate company marvel at how anyone could do such a thing. I wonder what she thinks of Jesus now?

When Christians work with each other and with the world, especially when we are speaking to unbelievers about their need for Jesus Christ and sprinkling the conversation with references to prayer and God's will, we should act with the utmost integrity. Two of Paul's most faithful converts were Aquila and Priscilla, a couple he worked for in the tentmaking business. They had observed his character in the workplace and wanted the Jesus he preached about.

What do you want to bet that Paul made top-quality tents? And Jesus undoubtedly made fine pieces of furniture growing up in Joseph's carpenter shop. If you are serving not only men but God in the workplace with love as your motivation, you will be inspired to do business more than fairly. You will also quickly acquire a reputation that all the money in the world cannot buy—and remove a stumblingblock from those who have not yet entered the Kingdom of God.

What to Do about Pharisaism in the Workplace

If you know someone who is making decisions in a pharisaical manner, why not talk to him about the fruit of his decisions? Such a person may live in a realm of religious denial, but before he damages anyone else, he needs to be confronted. Likely no one has ever challenged him gently about his behavior.

Explain to him how unbelievers may perceive the results of his decisions. Does he really want to give a bad testimony to those outside the Church? How will they view Jesus Christ after doing business with him? Will what he does make them want to know Jesus? Or will what they perceive as greed and manipulation drive them away, causing them to stumble over the sin in his life instead of over the Gospel of Jesus Christ?

It is better to suffer loss than have the cause of Christ driven through the mud. Paul wrote, "Respect what is right in the sight of all men" (Romans 12:17, NASB). Do things in a business deal or informal agreement that will leave others with a good taste in their mouths and even marvel at your fairness and desire for integrity. Better to go the second mile and take the hit than shame the name of Jesus Christ.

Jesus told us to "be wise as serpents and harmless as doves" (Matthew 10:16). He understands our need not to be taken advantage of. Pray about situations in your life and open up to wise counsel. Turn to a colleague with experience, sound moral principles and an impeccable reputation.

One Christian family called me to estimate the value of their home for sale. My broker and I assessed the value based on the market prices of comparable homes in the same neighborhood (the wise way to price property). This family had "heard a price from God," however—a price $20,000 higher than the top price their house could expect to fetch in the current market. Even though we told them that getting that price would be impossible, they considered such a view unspiritual.

So we listed the property at the higher price and advertised it during the high real estate season, employing every means we could to promote the sale. The high price they demanded resulted in not a single showing. Months later they took the house off the market, angry with us as though we were not doing our best. (The property has not sold yet.)

The fault lay not with us but with their inability to see they had not been listening to God's voice. But to their way of thinking, God was not directing them through reputable, experienced realtors.

James must have run into problems like these in the early Church. He was one for living out spirituality rather than talking about it all the time. A faith that does not produce fruit, James believed, is not real. His advice cuts to the bottom line of Christianity and tests us to see if our behavior is full of integrity and motivated by love. Here is James' prescription for determining if a matter in question is really wisdom from God:

> The wisdom that is from above is first pure, then peaceable, gentle, willing to yield, full of mercy and good fruits, without partiality and without hypocrisy. Now the fruit of righteousness is sown in peace by those who make peace.
>
> James 3:17–18

Why not write out this passage and put it by your phone? If you work in an office, put it by your business phone (not in unbelievers' offices or by the coffeepot!). Let it remind you to test all your decisions against the wisdom of God. Are you treating others as you want to be treated? Do you believe God will honor your integrity, even though it may cost you? (It may even cost you money.) Are you willing to put God first by being honest and kind, rather than holding up your superspiritual mask?

You may not be the richest man or woman in town, but when you lie down at night, you will be able to sleep because your conscience will let you. And chances are that people who know you will already realize you are a Christian without your having to distribute a single tract.

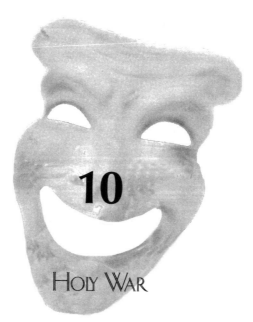

10

HOLY WAR

P hil had been a pastor for only several months when his church began to grow. Fresh out of seminary, he began to experience results with personal evangelism and door-to-door visitation that were almost miraculous. Phil had spent the extra funds necessary to do a little market research to discover the demographics of the neighborhood he had targeted for his new church. He also found out what people did not want in a church: boredom.

They did not have to worry about that with Phil. His services and sermons were far from boring. In fact, his enthusiasm in the pulpit was equaled only by his fearlessness at confronting issues. Phil could not stand "wimpy" ministers who soothed their congregations with sermons about love and unity while the world was going to hell. What people needed, he felt, was a no-compromise preacher who saw issues in black and white and challenged the congregation to action.

As soon as the church could afford it, Phil took to the airwaves to proclaim his messages, broadcasting for a full hour every afternoon an impassioned call to the citywide Church to rise out of apathy and give everything to following Jesus. After a few weeks on the radio, he began to confront the abortion issue head-on. Local elections were coming up and Phil saw the immediate need of making sure his candidates were elected. They were.

Phil's radio audience was growing and his church pews filling with Christians like himself who were tired of not affecting society. People saw in him the leader Christians in their city needed to change things. His church called for regular rallies and marches to oppose proposed ordinances and school board decisions that he deemed ungodly.

But Phil was not satisfied merely to speak out himself. He began telephone campaigns for causes he believed in, to enlist the support of other ministers and churches. One day, however, he was shocked to find a minister who thanked him politely for calling but did not believe it was his role as a minister to speak out on political causes.

That afternoon Phil took the disagreement before his radio audience. He called the minister and church by name and scolded them publicly for being apathetic and insensitive to the spiritual warfare going on in the heavenlies for their city. The switchboard at the station began to light up with callers reacting to his statements. Many congratulated him on his courage to speak out, but many were hurt that he had spoken against a minister with a reputation in the city for being gentle and devoted to unity in the Body of Christ.

When the other minister did not react to his attack, Phil kept on. "If we want revival in this city," he declared on the radio, "we have to see apathy for what it is, and vacate lukewarm churches who won't rise up in faith and act!" And once again he spoke out against the mid-sized church and pastor he had identified.

By this time ratings for Phil's radio program were skyrocketing. Each afternoon nearly every Christian in the city was tuning in to hear what inflammatory statement Phil would make against yet another church and its minister, whose only crime was failing to join Phil's fan club.

The Christian radio station, which was owned by a secular media franchise, saw Phil as their golden boy. They offered him a job anchoring their live talk show, which followed the airtime purchased by Phil's congregation. This gave him two solid hours a day to speak. Then a local television station invited him onto a talk show, where once again he denounced specific congregations he felt were not serving Christ passionately enough. Phil began to see his responsibility as a watchdog for the Body of Christ anointed to expose wolves in sheep's clothing.

Soon the local ministerium had had enough. They called the radio station asking for airtime to respond to Phil's attacks. The local TV talk show invited them to appear with Phil for a live confrontation in front of a studio audience. But the ministers were no match for Phil's wit and youthful enthusiasm. Many of the members of their churches began to leave and denounce them as "namby-pamby, milquetoast, mush-mouthed Pharisees"—a phrase Phil had coined to incite the Body of Christ to action.

Then he began to preach about revival. Soon, according to Phil, only he was anointed to bring revival to the city. God would not visit churches that refused to take a stand on issues. They were "stained-glass tombs."

Members of Phil's church, growing weary by this time of a constant diet of issue-oriented preaching, began to drift across town to a new church starting up. When Phil heard about it, he sent some of his elders to the meetings to check them out. Not wanting to disappoint him, the elders told Phil what he wanted to hear. There were "unusual" things happening there.

Once again Phil went on the attack, this time against the growing church. He denounced the pastor as a false prophet, and the emotional responses of those attending the meetings as heretical. He went so far as to obtain tapes of the meetings and play sound bytes taken out of context to prove that the pastor was involved in "gross error." But many of Phil's listeners, becoming curious, attended the meetings to see what was going on. The crowds at Phil's church began to diminish considerably.

Phil continues to rant and rave on the air. Most of the unbelievers in town think he is a phony media evangelist out to make a dollar. Many Christians believe God sent him to the churches with a ministry of discerning spirits to protect them from deception. Other members of the Body of Christ, however, do not see Phil's verbal abuse and arrogant attitude as Christlike. What will become of Phil, they wonder, if God ever allows him to reap what he has sown?

Sons of Thunder

What is wrong with Phil infected two of Jesus' dearest disciples before the Lord corrected them. James and John, the sons of Zebedee, were apparently enamored of the ominous qualities of God they had read about in the Law of Moses. Perhaps they were taken with the Scriptures that equate God's voice with the sound of thunder. Jesus must have found their intensity amusing enough to give them a nickname—*Boanerges,* or "sons of thunder."

When the people of Samaria refused to give Jesus and His disciples lodging for the night, since they were Jews headed for Jerusalem, James and John suggested they call down fire from heaven to consume the people for rejecting Christ.

The idea of calling down fire was scriptural, straight out of 2 Kings 1, in which Elijah called down fire out of heaven to consume two companies of fifty soldiers each that had come to escort the prophet to an audience with the king. Interesting how we can usually find a Bible verse to justify our anger!

But Jesus rebuked James and John: "You do not know what kind of spirit you are of; for the Son of Man did not come to destroy men's lives, but to save them" (Luke 9:55–56, NASB).

Perhaps this tendency more than any other causes sincere Christians to depart subtly from the primary goal of Jesus Christ—the salvation of the world—and get caught up in trying to force an unbelieving world to conform to Christian principles. The result is usually no more than a momentary victory against a floodtide of secularism, while it focuses the attention of unbelievers on the self-righteousness of Christians.

Holy War

In fact, trying to conform society to our beliefs is not a teaching of Christ at all, but more akin to a tenet of Islam known as *jihad,* meaning "holy war." This may sound like an outrageous comparison, but let me offer some background to explain what I mean.

Jihad implies not only the spread of the Muslim's religious beliefs, but also his personal battle against evil, which includes the righting of injustice. Islam began to develop as a religion during the seventh century after Christ, and has spread until it is the fastest-growing religion in the world today, expanding by an estimated 25 million people per year. Several governments of Middle Eastern countries, as well as governments in Asia, Africa and parts of Europe, have been taken over by Muslim factions seeking to establish their brand of social and economic justice, gain political control over societies and run them in accordance with the principles of Islam.

From its beginnings Islam has been known as an aggressive religion, which by the mid–700s had invaded the Middle East, northern Africa, Spain and part of France. In response to this threat, Christians were drawn offside during the eleventh century and launched the Crusades, their own brand of holy war to free the Holy Land from Muslim domination. Rather than accomplishing this end, the Crusades only convinced Muslims that holy war was the valid means of overwhelming society, and that Christians were as aggressive as they were. Christian teachings were quickly submerged beneath inflammatory language and battle, which claimed thousands of lives as intercontinental violence erupted in the name of Jesus Christ.

I have no objection if a civil government wages war to defend itself. But I wonder at the warlike emphasis today in the Body of Christ, and find little support in Scripture for our use of carnal methods (more about them in a moment) to force society to conform to our standards. Jesus rebuked James and John for such an attitude, indicating that their impulse to use the power of God to do violence in Jesus' name was born of a different spirit than the Holy Spirit.

The night Jesus was arrested, Simon Peter unsheathed his sword in an attempt to defend the cause of Christ, and sliced off the ear of the high priest's servant. Impetuous Peter, we say. But how often have we, like him, rendered unbelievers unable to hear the Gospel by forcing them to quarrel with us over a side issue? Maybe we should hear Jesus saying to us what he said to Peter: "Put away your sword." Recall how Jesus restored the servant's ear and surrendered to violent death at the hands of a deluded mob rather than violate His commission from His heavenly Father not to destroy men's lives but to save them.

Christians have been sorely pressed in our society in the past several decades with the appearance of demonic influences on every hand. Our government, in the face of a floodtide of immorality, has begun to accommodate the wishes of the majority it is sworn to uphold. The majority no longer values the life of the unborn child or seeks to make life easiest for the cohesive family. Just barely does the Congress hold onto laws protecting churches from taxation and other forms of government control. But are these threats any worse than the early Christians faced at the hands of the Roman Empire? Did Jesus or the apostles ever advocate fighting the battles of the Kingdom of God at the level of human government?

The Kingdom of God on earth has always been obscured from the bulk of society. Not even when Constantine baptized his army and warred under the sign of the cross did the real Gospel flourish. Instead, the cross became a front for the expanding political power of a human emperor. Every time the Gospel has been altered to fit the power-hungry goals of human beings, it fails in its spiritual mission to seek out the lost and bring them to the feet of Jesus Christ.

Internal Holy War

Not only do the natural aggressions of Christians show themselves in battling the ills of society, but they also surface in differences among the brethren. In the past several years, Christian denominations and organizations have made the pages of national periodicals with their internal holy wars. Fights have erupted over who should lead groups or which doctrines should be affirmed as correct. Books castigate ministers for differences in methods of spreading the Gospel, sometimes even implying that their methods are satanic in origin. Ministries are denounced publicly by other ministries that seem dedicated to purging the deluded from among us.

Our current form of *jihad* has captured the attention of the average Christian, creating in him or her an overdeveloped fear of deception, as though the Word of God and the Holy Spirit were not enough to protect from error. Is it now the function of ministries to act as the religious counterparts of *60 Minutes* to assure that the Body of Christ does not fall for error?

From the national pulpits of the religious media, the Christian of the '90s is told what to believe, then asked for a donation. The fact that money is being made at the expense of the reputations of other brothers and sisters in the Church, and unbelievers whom we are supposed to win to Christ, somehow escapes us as we surrender to our fear of deception. We do not notice that this fear is always followed by the urge to fight in the name of defending the Gospel. Then we begin to persecute what we do not understand.

Rather than vocalize our objections calmly and in a humble spirit, acknowledging the possibility of our own error, we resort to the use of loaded words like *false prophet* and *heresy,* when what is at stake would not result in anyone's eternal demise. We impugn the character of a ministry without complete investigation as though it were our righteous duty, and use guilt by association to influence the listening public to join the bandwagon of opposition. Soon we are holding inquisitions, officiating over kangaroo courts and drumming people out of our ranks.

Sometimes it seems that Jesus continues to suffer at the hands of the Pharisees. More than one sincere brother or sister has known what Jesus meant by the words, "They will make you outcasts from the synagogue, but an hour is coming for everyone who kills you to think that he is offering service to God" (John 16:2, NASB).

Embarrassing testimonies of our ecclesiastical mistakes litter the pages of secular and church history. It seems that every move of God persecutes the next, as the Almighty—to our unbearable chagrin—leaps out of our doctrinal boxes. In an attempt to force Him back in, we load our weapons and take aim at the brethren who just do not see things our way. Usually within the next decade we welcome them back into the fold as we realize they really did love Jesus after all; they just had a different way of showing it.

The Claims of Christ

All this zeal grieves the Holy Spirit and causes unbelievers to stumble over issues other than their need for salvation. Let's examine two important passages of Scripture to help people like Phil who are losing sight of what is eternally important in the light of the temporal.

Jesus' agenda transcends the temporal rise and fall of the rulers of this age—including the ones in control of religious organizations—and focuses on the eternal establishment of the invisible Kingdom of God in the hearts of men and women. Whenever this ground, the heart of a person, is won, many of the temporal goals of Christianity may be accomplished, while the Kingdom of God is enlarged to contain one more precious soul far more important to God than what is achieved by our human effort. Jesus' Kingdom is not spread by human weapons like political agendas and the use of control and manipulation to achieve His ends.

Matthew, one of His followers, noticed Jesus' aversion to demonstrations and zealous causes as a sign proving that He was the promised Messiah. Matthew quoted the prophet Isaiah:

> "Behold! . . . My Beloved in whom My soul is well pleased! I will put My Spirit upon Him, and He will declare justice to the Gentiles. He will not quarrel nor cry out, nor will anyone hear His voice in the streets . . . till He sends forth justice to victory; and in His name Gentiles will trust."
>
> Matthew 12:18–21

Jesus did not employ bandwagon techniques to influence the masses to do His bidding. He did not cry out against injustices perpetrated by the Roman government (including the slaughter of innocent children), seek to overthrow their political power (as the zealots of Israel expected Him to do) or judge them for their worship of false gods.

The apostle Paul, picking up the tune, admonished the early Christians against the use of carnal weapons in casting down principalities and powers (see 2 Corinthians 10:4). Weapons of the flesh always cry out, lifting up their voices in the streets because they see their enemies as flesh and blood, and miss the fact that the real enemies are spiritual forces that blind men and women and can be destroyed only by anointed, humble praying.

Jesus also promised, "Blessed are the meek, for they shall inherit the earth" (Matthew 5:5), not, "Blessed are the aggressive and warlike, for they shall accomplish My agenda." His passion and death testified how much He believed these words. His belief in His own resurrection caused Him to triumph God's way as He resisted the temptation of Satan throughout His life to supplant the kingdoms of this world by natural, demonic means (see James 3:13–17). Instead His method involved surrendering to death, knowing it was the doorway to eternal life.

When Jesus stood in Pilate's hall, the Roman governor asked Him if He was a king. Jesus' reply set the agenda for the Church: "My kingdom is not of this world. If My kingdom were of this world, My servants would fight . . . but now My kingdom is not from here" (John 18:36).

Until Jesus comes again, servants of His Kingdom are to pursue His ends without fighting, quarreling, lifting up our voices in the streets, overthrowing governments or persecuting and killing errant men and women. *Jihad,* in other words, is not a tenet of the Christian Gospel. Instead the Scriptures teach, "Malign no one" (Titus 3:2, NASB) and, "Love your enemies . . . do good to those who hate you, and pray for those who spitefully use you and persecute you" (Matthew 5:44). The chief sign that a conflict has degenerated from spiritual to natural is behavior contrary to these admonitions: attacking others verbally, despising our enemies, finding ways to control and manipulate them, persecuting them in return for the evil they have done us.

Why is it so difficult to stay in the Spirit about our differences?

The Real War

A Christian still has natural impulses. These, according to Paul, have the capability of warring against the work of the Holy Spirit in our lives. But as our minds are renewed to view things through God's perspective, we are lifted above the earthly skirmish to see the accomplished victory of Christ on Calvary as the deciding battle in the war against evil. If we believe Jesus has already won, we will enter a place of rest in which we do not have to strive against others, but conquer our spiritual foes with gentle meekness and weapons of love and mercy.

Sometimes the Lordship of Christ in our lives calls us to appear weak to others or as though we have been bettered in an argument. This cuts against every shred of human pride and the need to control—the two greatest natural forces within that resist yielding to the Holy Spirit. *We want to be right* at the expense of the reputations of others, as though they were a threat to us anyway. *We want to be ahead,* as though the assumption of earthly position meant anything in God's Kingdom. Jesus' teachings about leadership involve humility and servanthood—antithetical to human views of leadership won by defeating the opposition.

The greatest battle for the Kingdom of God is the battle the Holy Spirit wages within each of us to do things His way, not ours. Depending on the depth of our faith in God, we will surrender to His ways, which may lead us through paths of humiliation and seeming defeat while we utter not a word in our own defense.

Is there ever a time when a Christian should speak out?

The issue is usually not *whether* to speak out but *how.* Should we employ the methods of the world to get our points across? Should we boycott, take to the evening news and denounce the opposition angrily as though they were a true threat? No. Uppermost in our thinking should be the fact that they are no threat at all. At stake is not the issue for which they clamor. The truth is, their side has lost the final battle already and they are in danger of losing their chance to be saved if they do not come to know Jesus Christ. Such a revelation should provoke us to prayer and gentle earnestness, rather than the need to quarrel over the presenting issue.

Should we speak out against social injustice? Only with a spirit of meekness and gentleness. We should expect that if God is warring alongside of us, we do not have to resort to a power struggle to win, since God has already won. When a society refuses to turn, we should maintain our focus on the individual souls of men and women rather than on the current issue of the day. And sometimes, like Jesus, we may die unjustly at the hands of society.

The Bible is aggravating in its failure to rattle the saber for causes, including the destruction of slavery. The Scriptures admonish the Christian slave to contentment, not angry resentment. To the twentieth-century Christian, silence on such an issue is akin to heresy. Because we are Christians, however, and for us to love is supreme, there are times we may point society to a higher way. But our position should fall short of angry denunciation and the figurative shedding of blood. As a result of our interjecting righteousness into the arena, society may fight it out, while our responsibility as prophets has been discharged and the blood cleansed from our hands.

Francis Schaeffer, the evangelical philosopher, wrote this in his essay "The Mark of a Christian":

> What divides and severs true Christian groups and Christians … is not the issue of doctrine or belief that caused the differences in the first place. Invariably, it is a lack of love—and the bitter things that are said by true Christians in the midst of differences.

Right doctrine or opinion, according to Schaeffer, is not enough for Christians. Speaking out must also contain observable love.

So What's a Christian to Do?

Not long ago a minister called Bill and me on the phone to enlist our participation in an organization opposing abortion rights. Only the week before a doctor who had performed many abortions had been shot dead outside a clinic in Florida. I commented to the pastor how awful such an act was, and how damaging to pro-life causes.

"Well, he was killing innocent babies," he responded. "What's the difference?"

In his mind, the anti-abortion extremist was justified in committing murder by the doctor's guilt. To him murder was a justifiable act of holy war. The cause had become an obsession. Killing the doctor was a service to God and to righteousness since, in this minister's view, God was obsessed with eradicating evil at any cost.

Phil, the radio preacher, also sees the cause as primary and the methods of implementing the cause as secondary. Far from having the heart of Jesus, Phil's attitudes have proceeded from the same spirit that temporarily deceived James and John to want to call down fire from heaven.

There is evidence that Saul of Tarsus was also infected with this fleshly zeal when he first came to Christ. In Damascus he proceeded to take on his former cohorts on the Sanhedrin, this time convincing the members of the council that Jesus was indeed the Christ. Returning to Jerusalem, Saul continued to confront the Hellenists openly until they attempted to kill him. The brethren took him to Caesarea and shipped him off to his hometown of Tarsus.

The next verse is almost humorous: "Then the churches throughout all Judea, Galilee, and Samaria had peace and were edified" (Acts 9:31)—as though Saul's impetuosity and immature understanding of the nature of Christ had been doing more harm than good to the Church. In the name of defending the Gospel, he had been doing little more than engendering controversy and provoking needless persecution for the Church. He was a Christian in his heart, but still a Pharisee in his methods.

Ecclesiastes 3:7 says there is "a time to keep silence, and a time to speak." Finding the difference is not easy. But one sure sign it is *not* time to speak is the presence of anger, regardless of how righteous we feel our anger may be. James was familiar with the tendency to right wrongs out of anger. "The anger of man," he wrote, "does not achieve the righteousness of God" (James 1:20, NASB). Better to calm down and determine if God wants you to speak out, or simply to pray. The urge to act may be born out of a sick need to right wrongs in order to give yourself a ministry or make yourself feel holy. This feeds that wrong spirit that infected James and John.

Phil's need to right wrongs came from feelings of worthlessness, which were fed by his sense that as a young minister he needed to prove himself "worthy" to the Lord and to the Body of Christ in his area. A subtle pride took him over at this point, as he began to consider himself more important than anyone else in the Church. His arrogance was really an overcompensation for feelings of insignificance.

Phil was also angry at having been the child of an alcoholic, and he was attracted to the ministry by the need to rescue others in order to feel good about himself. His anger against victimization was laundered and came out as righteous zeal, as he gave himself unreservedly to causes, until he lost sight of God's perspective of the cause in the divine plan. Phil began gradually to see life in the light of the causes he advocated. The cause of Christ had faded in importance.

Because love had not been worked into Phil's character, his methods were like those of the Pharisees and people in the world he opposed. He was often photographed carrying a placard, his fist raised, his face angry. He loved the spotlight provided by the causes he championed. Soon he could not function without a cause. Where none existed, he gen-

erated one, as he did with the new church that he condemned as being in error.

Beloved, can we refrain from using words like *false
prophet, deception, error* and *demonic* in reference to those
with whom we disagree? Can we speak gently and humbly
to our brothers and sisters, so that we may turn them around
rather than provoke them to anger? Can we entertain the
possibility that we, too, might be wrong in certain aspects?
Can we show the same love to the world, so that we do not
present Jesus as their angry judge and foe but rather as their
Friend and Savior? Can we, as mature Christians, be easily
entreated, sympathetic, kind to all and patient when
wronged? Or is there no longer a reason to act like Jesus?

In eternity the victory will be not that we got some point
across, or that we won some election, but that the way we
stood for truth encouraged the lost to hunger for the Kingdom that produces people like us, ruled by a Lord who loves
the lost enough to tell them the truth in mercy.

What Happened to the Sons of Thunder?

James and John received the rebuke of the Lord Jesus and
apparently got the message. James became the victim of the
holy war created by the Pharisees against the Christians, and
lost his life. The apostle John came to repudiate the spirit that
temporarily had controlled his thoughts. In fact, God had a plan
by which John would really call down fire on the Samaritans.

As Saul of Tarsus began persecuting the church at
Jerusalem and killing believers, Philip, one of the seven servants of the early Church, went to Samaria and preached
Christ to them. They began receiving the Gospel wholeheartedly. Signs and wonders confirmed Philip's message,
and the Samaritans repented of sin and trusted Jesus. The
church at Jerusalem, hearing of this, sent Peter and John,

who began laying hands on the newly water-baptized disciples to receive the Holy Spirit (see Acts 8:14–17).

John, who had wanted several months earlier to call down fire out of heaven to punish the Samaritans for rejecting Christ, suddenly found himself praying for them to be baptized with the Holy Spirit and with fire! Fire was consuming the Samaritans, all right—the fire of the Holy Spirit. How much higher are God's ways than ours! I wonder if John realized what he was doing as he was praying for the Samaritans. Was Jesus looking down from the Father's right hand, finding the incident more than a little amusing? John went on to live until he was more than 90 years old, and became known as the apostle of love instead of a "son of thunder."

Whether inside or outside the circle of believers, Jesus admonishes us to love. Loving is more than simply telling the truth. Speaking the truth in love means that we speak in humility without threatening the removal of approval or affection. It means we do not use inflammatory words or methods of manipulation.

The older I become, the fewer the causes there are that demand my opposition. Even within the church, most of the struggles seem petty and lacking in eternal weight. I do not want to err, but if I do, I decided long ago that I want to err on the side of mercy. The most Christlike people I admire are those whose focus is the simple Gospel of Jesus Christ. Like the apostle John, who knew and loved Jesus well, they maintain quiet confidence in the power of a God who is not only holy but loving.

If I am wrong, I want to be corrected by someone with mercy. I want to have confidence in the God who transcends the political causes and social injustices of any particular age. I want to devote myself to the positive agenda of the Kingdom of God, leading men and women to Christ rather than fixing the leaks of a society that will eventually fail. If you have another view, I want to love you, too, and trust that we can disagree and still see ourselves as members one of another.

Now let's see how a church overcomes an aspect of Pharisaism to cooperate with the redeeming power of Christ.

11

REPLACING LAW WITH GRACE

The phone rang one afternoon in January. On the other end was the voice of our dear friend Joe Spooner from Oregon.

"Well, Bill and Melinda," he said, "I just thought I had to call and tell you. I'm getting married."

But instead of sounding elated, he sounded troubled, almost afraid.

Joe had come to the Lord seven years before, during the summer we had had a beach ministry in North Carolina. That was the same summer Joe and his wife had been driving around the country on leave from their jobs looking for adventure, when suddenly they decided to come to North Carolina to attend the wedding of our mutual friends, Mary and Elliott Tepper. Elliott wanted Joe to stay with us. But when we took our first look at Joe, we did not know what to expect. He was six feet three inches tall with long hair and a mustache, wearing a gauze shirt, jeans and sandals. We could not help liking him instantly, but we also felt a little afraid; visions of drug busts filled our heads.

But during the next few days, Joe became hungry for the Lord. The day after the wedding, our friend Tim led Joe to the Lord in the living room of the beach house where we were staying. Bill baptized him in the ocean that very afternoon.

Within a short time Joe was on fire for the Lord. But as enthusiastic as he was, his wife was cold toward the Lord and toward Joe. She had followed him through Zen and the drug scene, but when Joe turned to Jesus, she turned away. Before their trip around the U.S. was over, she packed up and left him.

For months afterward, Joe believed she would come back. He knew God had been drawing her, too, and could not understand why she had not received Jesus yet. Perhaps with more earnest prayer, faith, patience and love, she would finally turn to the Lord.

More than a year went by. Then Joe got the news that she was filing for a no-fault divorce. His hopes for a happy Christian marriage were gone.

Amazingly Joe survived this trial of faith. Back in Oregon he began attending a small church where he was received and loved for the next seven years. Joe devoted himself to personal evangelism, leading many friends and co-workers to a genuine relationship with Jesus Christ. He became active in the church, immersing himself in the Lord's work. His association with many long-term Christians was exactly what he needed to get established in his walk with God.

From time to time he sent us taped letters to update us on his Christian walk. We always looked forward to hearing how the Lord was using Joe and filling him with hope and joy in spite of his loss.

But on the phone that day, Joe began to unfold a tale of sorrow. For several months he had been teaching a high school Sunday school class. In the next room a lovely Christian woman named Dorothy taught a junior high class. Although they had tried their best not to admit it to themselves, the attraction was there; they were falling in love. For the past several months they had been driving across town and meeting in parking lots so they could have dates for dinner where no one knew them. They continued to attend church faithfully, but finally decided they were in love and wanted to get married.

The reason they had kept their dating secret became evident. Joe's church did not believe in remarriage after divorce. Sure enough, when he broke the news to the pastors, in whose eyes remarriage was adultery, they were horrified that Joe could have allowed himself to be overcome with such a temptation, when the Scriptures forbade him to as long as his first wife was alive.

Joe and Dorothy were heartbroken. Dorothy had attended that church for nearly fifteen years, served God faithfully there and developed relationships. Joe had been overseeing the church's outreach ministry and had even filled the pulpit on occasion. Now they would be allowed to attend and to tithe, but no longer to minister. So they decided to cross the river to the justice of the peace in another state.

Joe told Bill and me on the phone that they were calling family members reluctantly and a few Christian friends to tell them. What should have been one of the happiest moments in their lives had turned into an ordeal that they now wanted only to survive. Joe sighed as he finished his announcement.

Then I heard Bill's strong voice on the other extension. "Joe, you can't get married at the justice of the peace! You're a Christian now. You should get married in church. Why not come out to Pittsburgh for the wedding?"

I could hardly believe my ears. Bill told me later he could hardly believe *his* ears.

We never expected Joe and Dorothy to do it. But getting married in a way that would honor the Lord was important enough for them to scrape their savings together, purchase bus tickets and ride a bus for four days and three nights just to get married in a church full of people they had never seen in Pittsburgh, Pennsylvania.

Meanwhile, at Church of the Risen Saviour, the next few weeks were full of feverish prenuptial activity. It was as though our entire congregation took on the role of father of the bride for a Christian woman they had never met. The church rented linen tablecloths and planned a formal wedding dinner. Meetings were held to plan who would give the bride away and how the service would be arranged.

Christians from outside the church caught wind of the instant wedding and wanted to help. Wedding bulletins were prepared. Virginia, a Christian florist, donated flower arrangements and bouquets. Another Christian made and donated a multi-tiered wedding cake. Two young women who had visited the church for the first time only the week before sat up for two nights making dainty ribbon roses to decorate the room. All this was to be a surprise for Joe and Dorothy, who would arrive a few days before the wedding for premarital counseling and last-minute preparations.

On the Sunday of the wedding, the church gathered early. People visited from other churches, too. No one was disappointed when Joe and Dorothy entered the room. The looks on their faces were worth the weeks of preparation. Joe and Dorothy were overjoyed that God had redeemed their lives with a pure relationship and brought them together in a way that honored Jesus Christ.

But to Dorothy it was even more special. Before Bill performed the ceremony, she shared with the congregation what it meant to her. For years she had decorated the hall of her own church in Oregon for nearly everyone who had been married there. She had spent hours on each wedding to make the hall as lovely as possible. Often she wondered if the Lord would ever send her a husband, or if anyone would decorate the church for *her*. When it happened that her church would not even allow her to be married there, she consciously gave up her dream of a church wedding. But God was more faithful than she had imagined. He had prompted people she had never met nearly three thousand miles from her home to prepare a church wedding for her and Joe. Her heavenly Father was blessing their marriage with a miracle of provision.

How happy I was for Joe and Dorothy! And I was very proud of Church of the Risen Saviour. It never entered anyone's mind that Joe and Dorothy should not marry, or that it would be anything but fun to give a wedding freely to a precious couple in need of encouragement.

Imposing or Untying the Burden?

Beneath the religious cover of legalism lies a virulent anger that searches for ways to deprive rather than bless. Legalism subtracts the redemptive power of Jesus Christ from what would otherwise be a happy scene, and substitutes a hollow shell of pharisaical form. All too often in Christian circles, the Scriptures are interpreted to bar the Lord Jesus Christ from any chance of exhibiting His power to take a life shattered by the evil intent of Satan and transform it for the believer's highest good. Nowhere in Christian tradition is this more true than with the tragedy of divorce.

There is no doubt God hates divorce. Joe hated it, too. In his eager, newfound faith, he trusted and believed as best he could that his estranged wife would return. But the Lord has given every person a free will; and Joe's first wife, rather than submit to the conviction of the Holy Spirit, went her own way, leaving Joe to face a life without a wife and children.

Dorothy, for her part, had waited her whole life for God to answer her prayers for a Christian husband. Keeping her commitment to Christ to remain chaste before marriage, she was determined to wait for the one God had chosen for her.

She devoted herself to the church, teaching Sunday school classes, taking kids on outings and planning programs, children's plays and Bible school activities. Dorothy and Joe were model Christians who intended to do nothing that would not glorify the Lord.

Should Joe and Dorothy have suffered because of the sins of his first wife? No. To think so, I believe, violates the Spirit behind the Word of God. The unbelieving spouse had departed of her own free will; Joe was free to do as God led him.

Jesus, the Redeemer

The new love relationship between Joe and Dorothy presented their church with an opportunity to demonstrate the power of Jesus, the Redeemer. *Redemption* means buying back what the devil has captured and ruined. Jesus Christ paid the price for our redemption with His blood. In order to be redeemed from the Law, all we must do is acknowledge our inability to redeem ourselves and throw ourselves on the mercy of the court. At this point Jesus rises to our defense and offers His blood, His life, in exchange for our debt. He becomes our Redeemer.

Jesus redeems freely with no strings attached. He gives us the free will choice of serving Him with our lives. Being able to choose prompts us to want to love and serve Him willingly, apart from a heavy sense of duty. Because Jesus is able to redeem our lives from hell, we trust Him freely and willingly to redeem situations in which the enemy of our souls has brought destruction and heartache. Then redemption does not apply only to eternal redemption from sin, but to many temporal situations in our lives on earth.

Unfortunately Joe and Dorothy's church allowed a rigid interpretation of Scripture—one I believe is erroneous—to rob them of the joy of seeing Jesus redeem to Joe the marriage Satan ruined. The unwillingness of that church to cooperate with God's redemptive plan almost robbed Jesus of the glory He would receive as the Redeemer of a sad temporal situation. And their fear of being untrue to the letter of God's Word caused them to violate the most important evidence of Christianity: showing love to the brethren. In their zeal to impose their no-remarriage rule, they created an impossible standard that Joe and Dorothy could not bear. By withholding their blessing on the marriage, they were as much as cursing it.

Joe and Dorothy have been able to forgive the church, understanding that long-held beliefs did not permit it to open its arms to them. But all-or-nothing, one-way-or-the-other, black-and-white thinking is characteristic of legalism. The problem with either-or thinking is that when "either" does not happen, we have only one alternative: "or." There can be no exceptions to the rules, no extenuating circumstances. We expect God to act in the ways we have determined He should.

When Joe and Dorothy decided to marry, the church had to enforce some sort of punishment. Defending its belief became more important than loving the people involved. The church found no recourse but to treat Joe and Dorothy as though they were sinning, although they were far from it. If the church had really believed they were sinning, why did it not ask them to leave, as Paul teaches in 1 Corinthians 5? Why was it content to allow them to stay and continue to give tithes and offerings?

The Impossibility of Keeping the Law

Law, because of its inability to apply to every person in every situation, is inferior to grace. In fact, according to Galatians 3:24, the Law is a schoolmaster to bring us to Christ and the knowledge that only He can save us. Keeping the Law entirely is impossible. Legalism works only one hundred percent of the time in an atmosphere in which we make no mistakes, no errors in judgment, no rebellious choices that damage our lives.

The Law shows us, then, that we cannot save ourselves or even be entirely obedient to God. But grace—the freely given, unearned favor of God—allows human beings the freedom to honor God's Word yet recognize the Spirit behind the Law. Mercy and truth always meet in Jesus Christ.

When Law is imposed without grace, there always follows an inconsistency, the need to make an exception. The legalist traps himself by his own attempts to enforce the rules rigidly on others, in spite of grace; when he begins (as Jesus accused the Pharisees) to "strain out a gnat and swallow a camel" (Matthew 23:24). The Law, meant for the rebellious man, winds up punishing the man who complies with it. It restricts his life while the lawless man continues doing his own thing.

As soon as Joe's church in Oregon made a hard and fast rule regarding remarriage after divorce, it was bound to be broken. A rule designed to bring about respect for marriage in a rebellious person wound up stifling the lives of Joe and Dorothy, and even trying to rob them of the way Jesus wanted to restore them.

The Law demands judgment. In order to escape from its judgment and be healed from the harmful effects of legalism, you must escape from its binding power. No one can live under the rule of the Law without breaking some aspect of it. It is almost impossible to be healed of the harmful effects of legalism and remain in the environment it has created. Joe and Dorothy had no choice but to find a church where they could be loved and accepted. The fact that they did not allow this experience to drive them away from the Lord testifies to the depth of their commitment to the Lord Jesus. Their attitude exhibited maturity. They knew that their presence in the old church would be offensive to the members and stifle their own Christian lives. Although they still love the people in the old church and long for their approval, they have left those matters to God and gone on with their lives.

Unfortunately, Joe and Dorothy's old church has been unable to accept them as a couple for fifteen years now. Their refusal to accept Joe and Dorothy's marriage has caused the church to view them with contempt. Judgment always leads to contempt. It also leads to all the harmful effects produced by the Pharisees that Jesus so adamantly condemned.

The prophet Isaiah understood that Israel's legalism had caused her to view other nations with contempt. When he called her to repentance, he wrote,

> "Is this not the fast that I have chosen:
> To loose the bonds of wickedness,
> To undo the heavy burdens,
> To let the oppressed go free,
> And that you break every yoke? . . .
>
> "If you take away the yoke from your midst,
> The pointing of the finger, and speaking wickedness,
> If you extend your soul to the hungry
> And satisfy the afflicted soul,
> Then your light shall dawn in the darkness,
> And your darkness shall be as the noonday.
> The LORD will guide you continually,
> And satisfy your soul in drought,
> And strengthen your bones;
> You shall be like a watered garden,
> And like a spring of water,
>   whose waters do not fail."
>
> Isaiah 58:6, 9–11

In the same chapter Isaiah condemned religious pretense as odious to God. His prescription for successful fasting said nothing about method or length, only the condition of the heart. Spiritual dryness, Isaiah was saying, is related to self-centeredness. It also results from placing heavy burdens on others and pointing an accusing finger at them for being unable to carry those burdens.

But if you condemn others, you condemn yourself, since you must place the same standards on yourself that you have placed on others. When you do so honestly, the Lord will show you situations in which you have been unable to perform at the level you expect from others. If you can learn to stop the cycle, healing will begin. When you realize God has accepted you with your shortcomings, you will not be so quick to condemn others.

The church that develops a legalistic, rigid approach to serving God usually winds up lording it over the flock of God, rather than serving it. But the humble church that represents not only the holiness of God but His love will find itself untying the heavy burden imposed on humanity by the Law, and by proclaiming and walking out a revelation of the grace that is in Christ Jesus.

Revelation of Grace

Grace, then, is the antidote for the leaven of the Pharisees. Grace is the revelation that all you have was given you freely by God. This includes your spiritual understanding, your ability to resist temptation, your talents and gifts, the fruit of your ministry, even your ability to stay faithful to God in times of trial. You have accomplished nothing on your own. That you have anything at all is because of God's mercy.

When we lose sight of this, we become hardened in our hearts toward others. Any unwillingness we have to dispense grace toward others who have wronged us—or even toward others whose lives we consider "spiritually incorrect" (perhaps the victims of divorce, or those who have remarried after divorce)—blocks us from feeling the approval of God. It may be someone we have not been willing to forgive, or a Christian leader who has disappointed us in some way, or a friend we believe has stumbled.

Maybe you need to apologize to someone for actions or attitudes that have caused you to feel superior toward him or her. Maybe you have been angry about someone's inability to perform to your standards. Maybe that person has done wrong. Is it your place to point it out? If you are angry about it, likely not. Jesus admonished us not to pick at the faults of others when we are blind to our own. Apparently this aggravates God and, when we cannot let go of our "right" to judge, keeps us locked up in debtors' prison.

During the past several years, I have become aware of how much I criticized others, especially other Christians. In an effort to soothe my low self-esteem, I noticed and pointed out people's faults. I criticized fellow believers for not being doctrinally pure or for being unable to control some besetting sin in their lives. Often I shook my head in disbelief and commented on what a shame this was; inside I was thinking how spiritual I was to have been able to escape these faults.

Once I decided, with God's help, to change, I was amazed at how often He pointed up my tendency to do this. Whenever He made me realize what I was doing, I would back up and apologize to Him. Mentally I would say something like this: "Lord, forgive me. I remember that I have said or done things equally distasteful to You, and You have forgiven me. I know I am blind to areas in my life You have yet to show me. I have no right to expect this person to think or behave the way I do. You are Lord; I am not." It also helped me to understand the emotional pain that had resulted in their struggles.

As I began to see in myself things that needed forgiveness, I started noticing my tendency to judge others gradually going away. Whereas before I had thought it my duty to observe shortcomings in other people in order to preserve my own doctrinal purity or holiness, I decided to trust God to deal with others. My mission to prevent them from making mistakes originated, I decided, from a false sense of responsibility. At times I was even interfering with the grace process in their lives. What they needed, I learned, was not my advice but my acceptance and love, regardless of the imperfection.

It is humbling to realize that you may be incorrect about a doctrinal perception and blind to a greater truth God is trying to show you. Sometimes there is a need for correction. But leave correction to those who have influence in people's lives. Believe me, you will be a happier person.

Had Joe and Dorothy's old church been able to cooperate with the Lord's redemptive work and left the judgment up to Him, it would have become a vessel of redemption. But to that church, it was more important to be right. When the need to be right supersedes our love of mercy, we know that Law has become more important to us than grace.

How can we give up our right to be right and stop being legalistic?

12

HOW TO STOP BEING A PHARISEE

A country-western comedy show I used to watch featured a routine in which a man in the doctor's office would move his arm back and forth and say, "Doc, it hurts when I do that!"

"Well," the doctor would reply, "don't do that!"

Positive Courses of Action

Recovering from Pharisaism may be as simple as not doing the things Jesus said the Pharisees always did. "Do not do according to their works," Jesus told the people (Matthew 23:3).

So let's take the things the Pharisees did that Jesus condemned, turn them around to positive courses of action and implement them in our lives. Rather than see them as "don'ts," let's examine four things we *should* do.

Untie Heavy Burdens and Help Remove Them

Rather than admonish others about what to do, help them do it. Legalists, like the Law itself, always remind others what they ought to do but do not provide adequate means. Christians already know what they should do. The Holy Spirit has done a great job of pointing up the need. What He wants us to do is show our fellow believers how, and help them do it.

Joe Spooner, for example, our friend in the previous chapter, found his first marriage ruined after he turned to Jesus Christ. When his first wife chose to end that marriage, the covenant was broken in the sight of God and society. This left Joe with a hopeless situation. Regardless of how much anyone wants a marriage to work, the only way it will work is with the full cooperation of both spouses.

Yet I have seen people in Joe's position counseled by well-meaning brothers or sisters to maintain their singleness at all costs. Ostensibly the rebellious spouse will be saved by the patience of the believing spouse. This almost never happens. And what these single brothers and sisters are being advised to do is a form of manipulation—guilt projection, eventually forcing the errant spouse to repent—while the spouse needs to respond not to a manipulative human tactic, but to the Holy Spirit's conviction.

But what if the rebellious party does repent? Was it our efforts or the grace of God that made it happen?

God, who creates all people with a free will, hates divorce. But He also hates to see the victimization of a sincere Christian at the hands of a rigid Law. What happened to Joe challenged the Christians in his life to help him find the redemptive will of God. Satan had presented him with a set of seemingly impossible circumstances. What Joe needed was a church that cared enough not to condemn but to affirm him, and submit to the Holy Spirit's supernatural working in the situation.

When the church in Pittsburgh saw Joe and Dorothy under a heavy burden—being condemned by their church and being forbidden to marry one another—they decided to untie the burden and lift it from their shoulders. Church of the Risen Saviour was full of many new believers aware of how much they needed the grace of God in their own lives. (Believe me, we have had our own issues of rigidity and legalism to overcome!) These believers, having experienced the grace of God's forgiveness, may have been more open to showing mercy. Rather than shun Joe and Dorothy, they helped to lift their burden, as they would have wanted it lifted from their own shoulders.

Legalists never envision themselves in a situation in which they need grace, but those situations occur. I have often seen Christians proud of their ability to lead a flawless life, who attribute their lack of pain to the fact that they have been obedient to biblical patterns, encounter a blemish in the family photo—a rebellious teenager, for example, who upsets their pristine image of a Christian home. Under the bondage of legalism, these believers see only two alternatives: either admit they failed and that they are being punished, or give in to shame and deny the problem, allowing it to fester in the darkness.

But there is another way. They can open themselves to grace by admitting it was only God's grace that gave them a good family in the first place, and only God's grace that can restore it. Looking for the grace of God lifts the burden of Law from your shoulders and from the shoulders of those around you.

Another aspect of Pharisaism that Jesus condemned is a desire on which legalism thrives.

Do Nothing to Be Seen by Others

Recently I attended a Christian women's meeting in which women in leadership were called on to pray, one after the other. What was supposed to take only a few minutes wore on to nearly two hours. I sensed an undertone of competitiveness as each woman tried to "out-pray" the last—sounding more intense, quoting more Scripture, showing more profound spiritual knowledge. Each prayer amounted almost to a mini-sermon.

It was because of such occasions that Jesus told the story about the Pharisee and the publican, both praying in the Temple. The Pharisee thanked God, in effect, that he did not really need Him; while the tax collector, in a prayer inaudible to those around, begged for God's forgiveness. The prayer of the publican, Jesus said, touched God's heart, while the prayer of the Pharisee went ignored. Why?

The Pharisee's prayer was a form of tokenism. He was more concerned with having prayed than with sensing his need for prayer. The only need he perceived was his need to have prayed, so that he could mentally check off *Daily Prayer* on his "Look-What-I've-Done-to-Earn-God's-Favor" list.

But spiritual disciplines were never meant for public display. Why do our public prayers have to benefit those who listen to us when we are supposed to be addressing the Lord? Why can't we simply talk to God and use "I" statements to express our desires and needs?

Not long ago I heard a message on the elaborate meanings behind the Lord's Prayer. The speaker was expounding on how the prayer that Jesus taught His disciples really models a higher, deeper way to pray, and that every phrase of that prayer reveals heretofore-obscured truths, the ignorance of which (he said) hinders our prayer lives.

While I am sure we still have a lot to learn about prayer, it seems to me that the Lord's Prayer reduces the complicated prayer habits and traditions of the scribes and Pharisees to a few simple phrases from the heart. It makes their religious formulas for getting God's attention seem futile. The word *prayer* itself makes that activity seem like a religious practice that we must study and learn in order for it to be effective. I don't know. Maybe we should just talk to God from the heart and forget "prayer."

I also wonder when we Christians drop comments into conversations about having risen early to pray or about how we are fasting. Not only are we disobeying Jesus' command to keep spiritual disciplines secret, but sometimes we are trying to intimidate others and make them feel unspiritual. It may be our way of saying, "Look how holy I am"—or even, "Look how much holier I am than you are."

If we have genuine faith, we will see the results of our prayers as the Lord who sees in secret rewards us. We do not need to let others know we "prayed the blessing down." Shouldn't we take joy in simply having spent time with the Lord, without caring that anyone ever finds out?

Stop Craving Honor and Position

The competitive spirit beneath Pharisaism always vies for attention, while real spirituality is content to remain secret and stay in the background. A case in point: the pastor of a small congregation in the Philippines about whom I saw a Christian news story. Barely able to afford food and shelter for his family, he spends his day ministering to the needs of the families in his church and praying for them. He takes pleasure in the joys of pastoring as Jesus meant it to be.

Our concept of spiritual leadership has degenerated into business administration. Most of the ministers I know are forced to conform to perfectionistic standards placed on them by businessmen in their congregations who feel that the Kingdom of God should be run like a major corporation. These parishioners rate success in ministry solely by the ability to promote church growth and administer a complex web of committees and departments. The atmosphere created is like that of the marketplace, in which the driving force is competition and the spiritual needs of the sheep are subordinated so that the giant, well-greased ecclesiastical machine we call "church" can roll on.

Dr. Joel Gregory, in his book *Too Great a Temptation* (Summit Group, 1994), describes the toll exacted from his spiritual life and family life trying to pastor his denomination's most prestigious mega-church. The church occupied a five-block area of downtown Dallas. The pastor's discretionary fund overseen by his predecessor was over half-a-million dollars. Joel had an $80,000 office decorated impeccably by a professional decorator in the congregation. At any time of day he could lift the phone and order anything he wanted from one of the church's staffed kitchens. He had lounge box tickets to the Cowboys games and other events at Texas Stadium. But his schedule was grueling, and it became impossible for him to do anything but play in the shadow of his predecessor.

As Joel grew disenchanted with the little empire he had been drawn into by his own desire to oversee, he reflected on his early pastorates in small congregations, and began to realize just how far he had come from Jesus' idea of pastor as servant. Eventually Joel resigned (to the shock of his denomination and the church world), and since then has become a cemetery plot salesman.

It makes me realize, contrasting the scenario of the Filipino pastor against the backdrop of the American mega-church, that on Judgment Day the pastor will probably have a front row seat next to Jesus, while some of the rest of us will probably need a pair of binoculars to see Him from the parking lot.

Much better to take the back row now. Stop craving position. Instead, take joy in responsibility. Titles and positions may follow, but if they do, you won't care. Taking the lower seat removes from you the pressure to perform, and tells people that the Lord's servant is a regular person like everyone else.

Perfectionistic ministerial standards, by contrast, often demand an aloofness that makes the minister seem otherworldly. Wearing a spiritual mask becomes second nature. Taking off the mask is the first step in humility. Having the guts to be yourself without religious pretense forces others to accept or reject the real you. While risky, this is better than having to act like someone you are not. It keeps you approachable—where people live. The vulnerability can be uncomfortable, but it is the only way to real peace.

It also helps you with the next item on the Lord's agenda.

Open the Door of the Kingdom to Others

The superspiritual mask can place a stumblingblock in front of others, making them feel that God is inaccessible, while Jesus came to make God *more* accessible. The way into a close relationship with Him is simple rather than complex. Forget about sermons and messages that make a relationship with the Lord seem out of reach. Find the simplest ways to describe what it is like to know Jesus.

One of the best ways to open the Kingdom to others is presenting Jesus as their Friend. "If anyone sins," John wrote, "we have an Advocate with the Father" (1 John 2:1). An advocate does not argue in favor of the prosecution, but the defense. Our Advocate, Jesus, does not point an accusing finger, but loves to forgive sin and develop a relationship with men and women, boys and girls. And He responds to childlike openness.

Becoming childlike opens the Kingdom of heaven to the beleaguered Pharisee tired of trying to prove himself to God and others. Think of positive childlike qualities—trust, simplicity, wonder, naïveté, freedom from worry, lack of inhibition, the ability to forgive quickly, the ability to be affectionate—and you will know what Jesus meant when He said that "whoever does not receive the kingdom of God as a little child will by no means enter it" (Mark 10:15). I believe Jesus was talking not only about the humility necessary for salvation, but about the qualities we need in order to receive from the Lord as long as we live.

Pharisaism infects the soul who is trying to know everything, refusing to trust, acting sophisticated, being unwilling to forgive. Pride creeps in, and every evil thing that goes with it. The Pharisee lives in a legalistic world of self-made religion, exulting in his spirituality, blind to his need. He does not even know how badly in need he is. Proud of his correctness, he has settled for a poor substitute for the real joy that comes with knowing Jesus Christ and being filled with His Spirit. He tries to shut off the Kingdom of God from others and refuses to enter it himself.

Contrast that with the story you are about to read about my friend Diane Sives.

Diane's Story

As a child Diane was spoiled by her father. He usually gave in to her, and even fought with her mother to make sure Diane got her way. By the time she was eleven, he realized he had created a monster. So from that time on, he refused to talk to her, communicating with her only in grunts (unless company was present) or relaying messages through her mother. Diane's parents were both moderate to heavy daily drinkers, although they both held jobs and went to work every day. They never took her to church. Diane and her brother went to Sunday school at their grandmother's Presbyterian church. She may have been the only Christian in Diane's life who prayed for her.

As a teenager Diane became active in the Lutheran Church and tried to live the Christian life—without much success. At fifteen she dropped out of church and, probably because of her hunger for security and affection, became involved with other teenagers who drank heavily and experimented with sex. Diane became pregnant, and married a boy at 17 whom she had known for several years. He went to Vietnam, and by the time he came back he had outgrown her.

In 1969 Diane's mother died of a blood clot to the brain, the result of an injury. Less than a year later, her father shot himself to death. From that time on, Diane, still searching for affection, gave herself to one man after another. She cannot even remember the faces of the forty or so different men she slept with. Between relationships she would review her mistakes mentally, swear never to make them again, then slip back into her old ways, unable to implement the changes she longed to make.

Diane began drinking steadily in 1977. After a relationship with an older man ended unhappily, she sought the affection of a man who was an alcoholic. Determined to rescue him and show him that life without drink was possible, she stopped drinking herself. After only a few days she realized she was craving alcohol. "You need AA," her friend told her. He was in a drunken stupor.

That night at Alcoholics Anonymous, Diane heard for the first time that change was possible. She intended to figure out the AA program and follow it on her own, but she was unable once again to implement change in her life. AA's idea of change, she knew, involved prayer. Diane did not want to pray because she no longer believed in God. Nevertheless, in the interest of cooperating with the AA program, she did pray: "God, I don't believe in You. You're dead; You died on the cross. But I'm going to pray to You because they told me to."

Diane had tried to talk to God in her adolescent days in the Lutheran Church, but it had been like talking to a wall. Now she asked God to show her if He was real. She asked Him to "do something"—anything out of the ordinary. To her astonishment, He did. She prayed again, and other things happened that began to make her believe God was really there.

In January 1982 Diane attended a retreat sponsored by another organization for recovering alcoholics. She had set aside this weekend to pray until something happened, so she went into the library of the retreat center and found several books containing devotional prayers. She tried praying them all. The next day, as she prayed a simple prayer from a prayer book for Catholic youth, she knew she had broken through and that God had heard her prayer. She turned her will and life over to Him, and knew He had accepted her.

Several of the people at the retreat whom she told about her conversion looked at her as though she had lost her mind, but Diane continued to talk about God.

That evening she had been asked to share her testimony with the group, which she did. Afterward she followed the group into the library, where a woman was teaching them how to participate in a New Age guided meditation. The woman dimmed the lights and had everyone lie down or sit on the floor, then close their eyes and visualize going to "wherever God was."

Some of the people around Diane had very negative experiences. But Diane, hungry for the one true God, suddenly saw a sheet unfold before her like a cloud and gather her up into it. She knew she was being lifted up into a realm with the Lord. When the leader told them they could return, Diane clutched at the sheet in desperation, determined that she had God now and would not let Him go. As the sheet came down with her, tears streamed down her face and she found herself exclaiming, "I've been filled with the Holy Ghost! I've been filled with the Holy Ghost!"

After the retreat Diane kept thinking about Jesus and imagining Him standing in the road wearing a white robe with sandals on His feet. She saw herself wrapping her arms around His ankles and holding on for dear life. "I was desperate to find Him," she says. "He was my only hope."

Diane found her way to a Spirit-filled Lutheran church and a Bible study. She began to learn what had happened to her at conversion. And for the first time, with God's help, she began to change.

Diane has been a Christian for more than twelve years now. When she first recounted to me her experience, she told me several well-meaning Christians had doubted that her experience was real. I did not. I remembered that Jesus showed the apostle Peter a sheet coming down out of heaven, full of unclean creatures, before He sent him to preach to the Gentiles (see Acts 10:9–16). To me it was as if Diane, searching desperately for the God who loved her, had taken desperate hold of the hem of Jesus' garment. Feeling unclean and unworthy, she had been caught up in the sheet, cleansed from sin and set down once again to resume her life filled with the Holy Spirit. Her childlike faith had touched God, who allows no obstacles to stand before the heart who wants Him desperately. In Diane's words, "He filled me with the Holy Ghost so that I would have the power to live and not die."

I love Diane's testimony because it is so *un*religious! What happened to her shows how eager the Lord is to respond to childlike faith. Diane's experience cuts across every rule of modern-day Pharisaism. It makes superspiritual people nervous because it suggests that Jesus Christ may have invaded a place many Christians think He would never bother to go, just to find Diane. Her powerful testimony of grace opens the Kingdom of God to people like her who feel desperate enough to grab onto Jesus and hang on for dear life. It demands that you let go of dignity and your religious mask in order to find true spirituality. It opens up all God's best to people the Pharisees would despise.

The Rest of Faith

The journey of the earnest Christian through the pitfalls of Pharisaism can bring him to the place where he finally deplores all his efforts to act spiritual. This, I believe, is what the writer of Hebrews meant: "He who has entered His rest has himself also ceased from his works as God did from His" (Hebrews 4:10). Spiritual pretense, along with every other work of the flesh, will ultimately fail. Unfortunately, many Christians may not realize they are playing a game of spiritual make-believe until they have lost all interest in the Lord or the Church. Some fall away and commit sins that have lifelong consequences. Some simply become hardened in their lack of enthusiasm, content to get by until they die or until Jesus comes.

My prayer is that you will see through Satan's calculated plan to use the leaven of the Pharisees to steal God's best from your life. You can find freedom—which you must protect by watching vigilantly over your heart, where the streams of life originate. But God will bring you to a place of rest, where a relationship with Him is no longer a struggle but a vibrant joy.

What am I saying? That we can find healing from the binding power of legalism as we return to the simplicity of knowing and loving Jesus Christ from the heart. In order to appreciate the simplicity of the Gospel, we must purge from our lives the leaven of the Pharisees, just as the Jews remove every crumb of leaven from the house and burn it before celebrating the Feast of Unleavened Bread. This is a picture of the purging of the sins of false religion and works from our lives. Only when we do can we appreciate how much we need the blood of Jesus, our Passover Lamb, to replace our pitiful, fruitless efforts.

Once the graveclothes of legalism are gone, we will understand the triumph of grace—God's unmerited favor. Unhindered by false religion, we will be able to serve the Lord with freedom and joy. And others will be able to get a better look at Jesus Christ, the treasure in our earthen vessel.

The next chapter is the most important one in this book. It exposes the most serious offense of Pharisaism. But I warn you, if you are satisfied with your spiritual walk, under no circumstances should you turn the page.

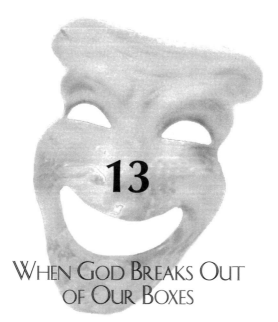

13

WHEN GOD BREAKS OUT OF OUR BOXES

My earliest recollections of praying for revival are the cottage prayer meetings my parents held in their home in the early '50s. I remember our house full of people—some sitting on crates for lack of chair space—asking God to visit our Baptist church with revival. Perhaps that is when the Lord put in me a desire to know Him. I received Jesus when I was eight years old and was water-baptized. From then on my spiritual search continued in waves of enthusiasm followed by ebbs of apathy until I was married and living in North Carolina.

When my friend Sarah Phillips told me about the moving of the Holy Spirit in the Body of Christ and issued what amounted to a call to prayer, hunger overtook me—hunger that did not diminish until I, too, had been filled with the Holy Spirit.

Embracing what God wanted to do in our lives proved costly to Bill and me. Many of our friends did not understand what was happening to us. Some thought we had gone off the deep end. Some hardened against us lest they be sucked into an experience they feared. Even after Bill finished seminary and we pursued the path of our denomination to the foreign mission field, we found we were already disqualified by our experience with the Holy Spirit—even though it was that experience that drew us to full-time Christian service.

When we took a small mission church in inner-city Pittsburgh, we thought it was only temporary until we could prove ourselves faithful enough for an appointment to foreign missions. Once again we were pursued by leaders in our denomination fearful about preconceived notions about charismatics—until finally our church voted to leave the denomination.

Twenty years have gone by. Only now is the denomination we left beginning to accommodate members who believe in the gifts of the Holy Spirit and who have been able to survive within its ranks. So I know what happens when God breaks out of our boxes. The Church experiences growing pains.

In that twenty years I, too, developed my own well-defined concept of what God would and would not do, based not on the dogma of my former denomination, but on charismatic tradition. I could quote chapter and verse on how God behaves in every situation. I had observed the gamut of evangelical and charismatic experience, but I did not like everything I had seen. Although love is the truest manifestation of Christianity, I did not see love in many charismatics who claimed prominent ministries or gifts of power. Nor had I myself grown this fruit sufficiently.

Ministries rose to prominence and fell because of sin. Doctrinal disputes or methodologies claimed our attention. In many church services purporting to be charismatic, freedom produced by informality substituted for spiritual liveliness. Many of us went through the motions of serving Jesus but were no longer enthusiastic about loving Him. What had happened to the revival? Had I been imagining the things I had seen God do in the '70s?

As I wrote in my book *Restoring the Wounded Woman* (Chosen, 1993), I became dry from living on a roller-coaster of hope and disappointment. I was compelled to die to my dream of ever seeing our church grow, since my sense of self-worth was tied to it. Bill and I must have been wrong to expect growth, or at least out of step with God's timing. I had to be content, even if God never fulfilled my expectations. To say I was dry is to understate my spiritual condition. I know what Jonathan Edwards meant when he described the spiritual condition of his town before the Great Awakening: "It seemed to be a time of extraordinary dullness in religion" (*Jonathan Edwards on Revival*, Banner of Truth Trust, 1994). But my heart longed to see God's power at work and feel His love in me again.

Rivers in the Desert

In September 1994 a letter arrived from our close friends George and Joanne Stockhowe, an Episcopal rector and his wife from Jacksonville, Florida, to share how God had met them at the renewal meetings being held at a church in Toronto.

We had heard about the unusual goings-on at the Toronto Airport Christian Fellowship (formerly the Toronto Airport Vineyard) and dismissed them as the latest fad scampering through the Church. For people to experience laughter in response to the Holy Spirit could not, I felt, be from God. Laughter was too contagious naturally to be a useful thermometer of God's presence. Besides, all revivals I had read about in church history were evidenced by tearful repentance, weeping and awareness of sin. Sin was no laughing matter. I was certain that upon hearing this "holy laughter" myself, I would know such a manifestation was improper—fleshly zeal at best, or much worse.

But when George and Joanne, who were not flaky, told us what had happened to them, we knew that our case against Toronto needed to be reopened.

Bill and I took a missionary expedition in October 1994 to England and Spain to scope out possibilities for our church's missions involvement and to fellowship with brothers and sisters over there. We were prayed for at the Chichester Christian Fellowship by British believers we had never met. One man felt God impressing him that what God had for us—what we had been waiting for—was behind a curtain about to open, and that we were about to see what God had planned for us all along.

After we had been in Spain for a few days, I had a dream one night. In the dream I was explaining to a couple how badly we needed revival. Suddenly the countenances of the couple changed to two men. One interrupted me and said, "Have I not promised you times of refreshing from the Lord?" As he said this, I felt overcome by the presence of the Lord. The next day the same sense of God's presence lingered so that I could not forget either the dream or the Lord's promise of renewal.

During the Thanksgiving holidays, Bill and I went to Toronto, wondering if we would find disappointment or that pearl of great price—the sense of God's presence in true revival. At the end of the first meeting, we were too dry and desperate to analyze. Guy Chevreau, author of *Catch the Fire*, had been speaking about how he had been touched in that church only months before and "drawn out to where I can never return."

How I, too, longed to be drawn out by God! But for years I had attended all kinds of Christian meetings, from the cerebral to the experiential, where I had been unable, practically without exception, to feel or experience anything. In fact, I had developed a secret sense of pride about not surrendering to anything that was not completely from God.

Still, Bill and I went forward to receive prayer. Guy prayed, "Let the rivers flow." He could not have known that the guiding Scripture of our ministry had always been Isaiah 43:18–21, in which God says, in part, "I will do a new thing. . . . I will even make . . . rivers in the desert." In spite of all my fears and reservations, I started to weep. And through the next three days and evenings, we began to receive glorious "soaking prayer"—extended times of prayer during which we simply "soaked" in the healing presence of Jesus.

The second night another pastor from the Toronto area prayed, "Come, Holy Spirit!" before his sermon, then commenced a message about Eldad and Medad prophesying in the camp of Israel. Suddenly the entire right side of the congregation erupted in laughter. There was nothing humorous about what he had said. Then I noticed that laughter was coming out of me. Later, during the prayer time, I was overcome by the presence of the Lord for the first time, and found myself lying on my back on the floor.

Hundreds of people lay on the carpet; many were still standing. I heard expressions of joy and laughter around me, but also weeping. Some were crying out under the overwhelming presence of God. Most of those apparently receiving touches from the Lord (Bill and I learned later) were pastors and their spouses from all over the globe—from Scandinavia to Borneo and Japan. More than a third of the audience was from Great Britain. (So much for myths about the reserved British temperament! Of all the seekers they seemed to be the hungriest.)

If I had any skepticism left about whether what was happening in Toronto was from God, it was laid to rest by the testimonies of those who had traveled thousands of miles to see if God was really there. Rather than magnifying the manifestations, as I had been led to believe, those testifying talked about how precious Jesus Christ had become to them since the renewal had begun.

Pastors making their second and third trips to the church recounted that renewal had spread to their own churches after their return. The same things happened at home as had happened in Toronto, and their congregations had been transformed. Some were seeing miraculous healings, the restoration of marriages, apathy being blown away. Former parishioners who had not even attended church only weeks before were now coming night after night, hungry for more of the Lord's presence in their lives.

By the last night in Toronto, I had been touched more deeply by God than I had been throughout the previous twenty years. He was breaking down my inhibitions, my disappointments, my false notions about how He moved, and bringing me to a place of humble receptivity.

Was it possible that the blessing would spread to our congregation back in the Pittsburgh area as well?

Back Home

The following Wednesday night back in our church, we called everyone together for a question-and-answer session. We gave everyone a chance to express concerns, which we answered as best we could. Then we sat in our seats in the sanctuary and watched the Holy Spirit begin to touch first one and then another. People we knew well began to weep. Some stood to their feet in worship. A sense of awe came into the room and began to hover over the group.

Over the next few weeks, although no manifestations had been modeled before our own church members, everything Bill and I had seen in Toronto began to take place at Church of the Risen Saviour. Passion began to be stirred for Jesus Christ. People testified about how the Lord was meeting them as they, too, received soaking prayer. Three members reported remarkable healings, which were later confirmed by radiologists. At least four women who had been suffering from panic attacks for more than a year were healed. Our praise and worship became more fervent and enthusiastic. Visitors hungry for more of the Lord began to come forward to receive prayer. Even facial expressions changed from furrowed brows to glows of peace.

In the following weeks, I surrendered again and again to soaking prayer at the altar of our church. Then one morning, as I reached for the Bible on my nightstand, I realized I was hungry to read it. It had been years since reading the Bible had been anything but dutiful. Passages in Scripture had reminded me what God was capable of, what God had done in the past and was not doing now. I was like a starving person who had missed so many meals that she had lost her appetite altogether. Now I was famished for prayer and His Word.

Much of what has been happening in me and in our church is different from how I have seen God move in the past. Some of the manifestations at the altar include not only "holy laughter" but shaking and falling down in the presence of God. Bill and I, in our desire to test everything against Scripture, have been amazed to find corroborations in the Bible we never noticed before, as God continues to move in people's lives. I have also been awed by the fact that my own Pharisaism almost caused us to miss the day of visitation for which we had prayed for nineteen years.

What Pharisees Miss

By the time Jesus arrived on the scene, the Pharisees already had definite ideas about what the Messiah would look like. Jesus did not fit that concept. They believed the Messiah would be a liberator, probably a Pharisee like themselves who would rise to prominence through their ranks and be anointed by God to deliver them from the Romans. Although the Pharisees expected the fulfillment of all the prophecies about the Messiah's triumphal return, they skipped the ones about Him as the Suffering Servant. They never expected a plain Man from Nazareth who would oppose their carefully developed religious system.

So the religious leaders opposed Jesus at every turn, denying that the power behind His miracles was anything but Satan. They accused Jesus of being blasphemous, demonic and heretical, and they saw to it that He was eventually killed. The Romans would never have bothered Jesus had it not been for the religious Pharisees, who found Him a threat to their existence. They actually preferred waiting for the Messiah to experiencing Him.

On Jesus' last trip to Jerusalem before His crucifixion, He wept over the city and said, "If you had known, even you, especially in this your day, the things that make for your peace! But now they are hidden from your eyes . . . *because you did not know the time of your visitation*" (Luke 19:42, 44, italics added). The people to whom Jesus had been sent did not realize He was their Messiah.

Failure to recognize the day of visitation is repeated by the religious in every generation who develop a carefully defined theological concept and persecute whatever does not fit. Church history reveals tragic examples of believers afraid of the Holy Spirit as He stretched and destroyed their theological concepts.

St. Theresa of Avila, an earnest, prayerful mystic who loved Jesus, opposed Luther and the Reformers vehemently. Words she wrote fueled the Spanish Inquisition. After Luther and Calvin prevailed with the Protestant Reformation, some of their followers drowned Anabaptists who believed in baptizing by immersion. Anglicans persecuted Puritans and the Methodists. The Pentecostal movement was derided by evangelical preachers like G. Campbell Morgan, who had been prominent in the Welsh Revival, as "the last vomit of Satan" (*Signs of Revival*, Kingsway, 1994). The Pentecostals, in turn, persecuted the Latter Rain Movement. Neither the Pentecostals nor the proponents of the Latter Rain, as a whole, embraced the charismatics of the '60s and '70s, regarding themselves as spiritually superior.

Sad to say, many charismatics and evangelicals today wind up persecuting whatever God does next. Most of the time those who persecute have no idea what they are doing.

But they brace themselves against the next move of God in their generation with careful, scriptural analysis, confident they are correct and certain that the new "revival" is nothing more than a fad or even a deception. But why?

Why Do We Miss the Day of Visitation?

There are a number of reasons we miss out on the works of God in our day. Let's look at six of them.

Cynicism

One of the principal reasons we miss what God is doing is cynicism. Some who love controversy and enjoy exposing evil begin to attack what the Holy Spirit is doing without even entertaining the thought, "But what if this is God?" I was vulnerable to this deadly attitude—though I understood the tendency of one revival to persecute the next—because I had grown weary.

But there is always a length of time between God's promise and its fulfillment. During this time, the external circumstances seem to say that what God has promised is impossible. We can come to think that we did not really hear from God at all; or, like Sarah and Abraham waiting for the promise of a son, that assistance is necessary to help God fulfill the promise.

Sarah waited for seven years (a great biblical number), then suggested that perhaps the promised son would come through Hagar, her Egyptian slave. God did not withhold Isaac from Sarah and Abraham after they attempted to fulfill the promise on their own, but neither did He allow Ishmael, Abraham's son by Hagar, to take Isaac's place.

What God does is pure—untainted by human effort. But we, like Abraham and Sarah, have given birth to "Ishmaels" that have the capacity to resist revival.

Unusual Doctrines

During the periods between revivals, many personalities enter and leave the "platform" of the Body of Christ. Unusual doctrines surface; different emphases take center stage. Sincere defenders of the faith need to challenge these doctrines (to which believers without sound biblical faith are vulnerable) in order to preserve the simplicity of the Gospel.

Anything that would subtract from the deity of Christ and the power of the Holy Spirit must undergo scrutiny.

"No More Miracles"

A third reason many of us miss the day of visitation is a widely accepted doctrine in the Body of Christ called cessationism, which proclaims that God no longer works miracles as He did in Bible times. This doctrine has caused many to miss or resist the moving of the Holy Spirit.

Jack Deere, a former professor at Dallas Theological Seminary, wrote in his book *Surprised by the Power of the Spirit* (Zondervan, 1993), "There is one basic reason why Bible-believing Christians do not believe in the miraculous gifts of the Spirit today. It is simply this: they have not seen them." Jack Deere realized that for years he based his theology on his lack of experience, rather than on the Scriptures. He was surprised to find that miracles were still happening. And when he realized that the power of God was still at work, his life changed.

Defending the faith can lead any Christian, without realizing it, to the pharisaical tendency to suppress what is real. But when we limit what we think God is capable of to our experience, we reduce Him to the size of our own brain.

Hopelessness

Some believers become discouraged during severe trials of faith and succumb to hopelessness, which can cause them to miss their day of visitation.

During the periods between revivals, many who have experienced a touch from God are tested through trial and heartache. Many a sincere Christian has found himself on a roller-coaster of hope and disappointment. As hopes rise to meet every problem with faith, a crisis develops, and then—when the divine solution does not seem forthcoming—disappointment. Sometimes the emotional devastation is so great—perhaps sickness or financial setback or the death of a loved one—that the believer loses hope. Emotions like shame and fear set in; feelings of despair may drive this believer to the brink.

Other believers develop substitutes for the moving of the Holy Spirit, in the form of programs and other stop-gap measures, to hold themselves together. Still others give up altogether and go back into the world. In any case, when a real move of the Holy Spirit comes, believers who have lost hope are afraid to examine it for fear of being disappointed once again.

They are like the disciple Thomas after the resurrection when he was told of the meeting in which Jesus had appeared. Jesus had shown those disciples His hands and feet. He had eaten with them and breathed on them, commanding them to receive the Holy Spirit. He had charged them to forgive others and given them the power to do so.

Thomas had not been there. And when his friends told him what had happened, he did not buy it. His faith had been too weakened by the crushing blow of Jesus' death for him to accept that his Lord was alive. So Thomas told them that unless he could see Jesus himself, he would not believe it.

Tradition

Our initial human response to change is almost always negative. We are told that a person will not replace an old concept with a new one until he has heard about it nearly thirty times. It is that difficult to break tradition. Sometimes the most faithful have the greatest difficulty. This happens when God pours Himself out on a group we did not expect or in a way we would not have chosen. At this point, tradition becomes the enemy of revival.

Jesus scolded the Pharisees, "You invalidated the word of God for the sake of your tradition" (Matthew 15:6, NASB). The Pharisees knew the Scriptures by memory but missed their day of visitation, not even recognizing Jesus as the Messiah when He came and stood before them. No wonder the apostle Paul wrote that "the letter kills, but the Spirit gives life" (2 Corinthians 3:6)! It is possible to know the Bible thoroughly and miss God. The problem is not the fact that an event is not biblical, but the fact that it is not traditional.

Tradition thrives on the security of sameness. Sameness causes what was once alive and vibrant to degenerate into dead orthodoxy. Regardless of our Christian denomination or affiliation, we have all experienced worship services in which it seemed that everyone was going through the motions. We could hardly wait for the service to be over. As revival wanes, what began as spiritually alive falls into apathy.

Tradition that interferes with revival may be perpetuated by our elders in the faith. Sometimes in the interest of providing spiritual protection, they wind up quenching the Holy Spirit. Jesus rebuked the Pharisees for traveling around the earth to make one proselyte, then turning him into a worse child of hell than they were (see Matthew 23:15).

Some worship patterns are based more on habit than on Scripture, and we can miss what God is doing when it does not fit our liturgy. Characteristically tradition exists to preserve the purity of the faith, but inevitably it winds up resisting the change that comes with revival. God breaks out of the traditional mold whenever people's spiritual needs are no longer being met. Every move of God, therefore, seems to manifest unusual signs and wonders. Whenever God begins a new day of visitation—as he did in the days of Wesley, Whitefield, Finney and Jonathan Edwards—the meetings seldom conform to traditional concepts of what "church" has come to mean. All those revivalists reported accounts of people falling to the floor, weeping loudly, losing muscular control (getting "the jerks") and other unusual manifestations. In addition, as God pops out of the traditional boxes we have squeezed Him into, He usually highlights an area of Scripture we either dismissed as not for our day or ignored altogether.

The Azusa Street revival of the early 1900s sparked controversy in the evangelical camp when speaking in tongues was poured out as it had been on the Day of Pentecost. At the time tongues-speaking was criticized as satanic and divisive; but the fruit of a century of Pentecostalism has been the spawning of churches all over the world and a fire for God that has never gone out, even in the driest times of this century. Those who know Pentecostals know they love Jesus Christ and are devoted to the Scriptures and personal evangelism. In fact, Pentecostal and charismatic churches are the fastest-multiplying Christian groups in the world.

In the 1960s a Pentecostal outpouring began to occur among Roman Catholics and Episcopalians. But a pharisaical attitude began to develop among both classical Pentecostals and evangelicals. The fact that Catholics were receiving manifestations of the Holy Spirit was enough for some conservative Christians to declare that the entire move must be satanic, since the Roman Church differed in part of its understanding of salvation. But fellowship with those who had received this outpouring revealed that they had turned from sin, loved Jesus Christ and were filled with the Holy Spirit. This was hard for evangelicals to take, since it nullified the need for anyone to become evangelical in order to be considered saved. Our tradition suffered a tremendous blow. But the Gospel did not suffer. The Holy Spirit moved into places we had given up as hopeless and caused the good news of Jesus Christ to flourish—including in the mainline denominations.

Fear

One final reason we do not recognize the day of visitation is that those we respect may not have entered in, and we fear the loss of their approval. Even when we know that some renewal work is from God, we can be prevented by the fear of man from enjoying the day of visitation.

Christians these days are seldom burned at the stake for embracing a move of the Holy Spirit; but fear of lesser repercussions can quench the moving of the Spirit in our lives. A layperson may be afraid to be considered a fanatic or to be judged for stepping beyond traditional bounds. A pastor may fear losing his pension or ordination papers. A ministry leader may be afraid of losing financial support. Any one of us can come under pressure to stop what may cause controversy, even if it is the real moving of the Holy Spirit.

During times of renewal, people frequently say things like, "If this were God, it wouldn't be divisive." But the Reformation was divisive. Jesus declared He "did not come to bring peace but a sword" (Matthew 10:34), and that "a man's enemies will be those of his own household" (verse 36). Sometimes these enemies are of the household of faith. The true revivals of Church history were always met with violent persecution by those in the world and in the Church.

Saul of Tarsus became perhaps the greatest apostle and the most effective proponent of Christianity, but not before he persecuted the Church violently. Under the spell of religious tradition, he entered the houses of many Christian families in Jerusalem and dragged men and women off to prison—some even to their executions. His opposition to the move of the Holy Spirit in the early Church was born out of pharisaical tradition and out of the fear of deception it spawns. Imagine the emotional shock of Saul's Damascus Road confrontation by Jesus Christ Himself! It is evident that Saul never got over it, nor the fact that he had persecuted the Lord he came to love. It humbled him for the rest of his life.

The fear of deception is not discernment, but often it masquerades for it. When Christian leaders who ought to recognize a move of the Holy Spirit begin to condemn it as heretical, evil or even demonic, it ignites in many Christians a fear of being deceived. If any fleshly excess occurs, *all* aspects of the moving of the Spirit can be called into question and summarily condemned.

The fear of being deceived can become a counterfeit for true discernment and actually cause you to become deceived. This fear is born of fleshly hypervigilance and can result in straining out the real Jesus in an effort to protect yourself. In recent years the Body of Christ has been told so often about the possibility of deception—and that unless we are careful enough, we will fall for something false—that many people have come not to trust any pastor or minister, or even the Holy Spirit, who is sent to lead the believer into all truth. We are making the same mistake Eve did when Satan told her that eating from the tree of the knowledge of good and evil would improve her discernment. Instead, it blinded her to the true God.

Some people think God is out to trick them, and that, unless they are careful, they will fall into error. But childlike faith—so necessary to receive anything from God—is stifled in such an atmosphere. Sheep must be able to lie down in green pastures, and will not lie down so long as they perceive any threat of evil. But ask yourself: Is God so abusive that He would allow us to be tricked with the false when we are seeking Him desperately? If you ask the Father for the real Holy

Spirit, He will not give you a snake instead of a fish (see Luke 11:9–13) or allow you to receive anything false.

Then there is the fear of emotional displays. When one of the Pharisees invited Jesus to dinner, a sinful woman brought an alabaster box of costly ointment. Crashing the banquet, she proceeded to wash Jesus' feet with her tears and wipe them with her hair. She kissed His feet and anointed them with the fragrant oil. This display of emotion embarrassed the Pharisee who had invited Jesus to his home.

Love is an emotion, but when it comes to Jesus, we have been conditioned against any expression of exuberance. If a person becomes (by our own standards) too "emotional"— like the Pharisee uncomfortable with the woman's display of devotion to Jesus—we conclude that he has transgressed "normal" bounds, that he must be in error. Tradition, then, dictates how we are to respond to God.

But if we examine the Bible, we see that when the Holy Spirit came, there was dramatic evidence of His presence. Throughout the book of Acts, those touched by the Holy Spirit exhibited strong emotions like joy, even to the point of seeming inebriated (Acts 2:13). Jesus Himself "rejoiced greatly in the Holy Spirit" (Luke 10:21, NASB). The Greek word in this passage, *agalliao,* means "to rejoice with great leaping about." If Jesus can express this kind of emotion, we can, too.

In Revelation 2, the church of Ephesus was reproved by Jesus Christ for leaving her first love. She was commended for perseverance, works of service, enduring persecution patiently and exposing false apostles; but her love for Jesus and the childlike trust so necessary to enjoying Him had faded away. Losing love for Jesus is perilous. He told the church at Ephesus that her lampstand would be removed unless she returned to her passion for Him.

Can you see yourself in Scriptures like that? If so, how can you regain your passion for Jesus and get back to where you feel the presence of the Lord again? Do you long for your own day of visitation? But how can you know whether God is moving in a particular situation, or if it is the flesh or even Satan?

What to Look for If It's God

The only way to know whether an experience is from God is by the fruit: *Does it bring you closer to Jesus Christ?* Any number of unusual manifestations can occur when people experience the presence of God. Crying is often the one we look for, but many in Bible times who experienced the Lord's presence had a different experience, including joy, laughter, shaking and falling down in His presence. These are all biblical responses to God. Some people have no emotion initially, yet experience a dramatic change reflected in their behavior afterward. I have heard it said that if people are afraid, the experience cannot be God. But if that is true, why did every angel who appeared to someone in the Bible have to say, "Fear not!"?

What happened to Peter, when he was called by God in a dream to preach Christ to the Gentiles, demonstrates how we are to discern whether something is truly from God.

Identify the Fruit

Peter saw a vision of a sheet unfolding before him filled with unclean creatures. A voice said, "Rise, Peter; kill and eat!" (Acts 10:13). God was actually asking him to violate the Scriptures, as well as traditions from the Law of Moses that he had observed all his life. He saw the vision not once but three times, and each time replied, "Not so, Lord! For I have never eaten anything common or unclean" (verse 14). His fear of deception was firmly in place. But each time the voice replied, "What God has cleansed you must not call common" (verse 15). Here was a vision that had no scriptural basis, yet was obvious to Peter.

Afterward three men from the home of Cornelius, a Gentile centurion of the Roman army, stood at his door. Cornelius had been told in a vision of his own to send for Peter, and was even given his address in Joppa.

Peter went with the men. As he began to preach in Cornelius' home about Jesus, the Holy Spirit fell on all of them and they began to speak in tongues, as Peter and the others had when they first received the Spirit (see Acts 10:44–46).

God was doing something new with Peter and Cornelius. He moved upon both men supernaturally and changed Peter's doctrine in the process. The early Church had already identified the audience for the Gospel: the Jews. Peter had defined the conversion experience: Repentance, water baptism and receiving the gift of the Holy Spirit, in that order (see Acts 2:38). This had happened throughout Jerusalem and in the Samaritan revival as well. Peter was used to seeing God move on certain people—the Jews—in a certain way.

So when Gentiles at Cornelius' house began to receive the baptism in the Holy Spirit without praying the sinner's prayer or being baptized in water, he was incredulous. Happily for the Church ever since, Peter was open to change. As he related the incident to his brothers in Jerusalem, he concluded, "Who was I that I could withstand God?" (Acts 11:15–17). He had seen the Holy Spirit being poured out not on Jews but on Gentiles, with the same manifestations as at Pentecost, but in a different order. God had broken out of His box. And Peter did not try to force Him back in.

How did Peter know the Gentiles' experience was genuine? Because of the fruit. Cornelius and his household were devoted to Jesus Christ.

The fruit of the Holy Spirit is always the exaltation of Jesus Christ to His rightful place as Lord. Signs and wonders call attention to the message. Peter knew that the vision was of divine origin, the tongues were from the Holy Spirit and the

Gentiles had become Christians by the fact that they all professed belief in the Lord Jesus Christ. In judging whether any move is from God, look for people turning to Christ or being renewed in their love for Him.

Know You're Hungry

Inevitably a person opens up to revival only when he or she is hungry enough.

My initial reaction to what I had heard about the church in Toronto was negative: I doubted that the manifestations to be seen there were biblical. I was ignorant of what Church history has to say about such manifestations, even though I had studied revival thoroughly. I also had a fear of emotional displays and, to some degree, what other people would think. Nor did I want any more spiritual disappointments.

But in the end I was so hungry that I became like the wretched people invited to the banquet in Jesus' parable to replace the guests who refused the invitation. I could not stand another minute of dryness. What if this revival was from God and I missed Him because I was too proud or cynical or legalistic to notice? I needed Him so badly that I lost my dignity and sense of etiquette. And when I saw that the banquet was real, I tore into the table spread before me like a hungry beggar. It did not matter if in the process I fell on the floor or laughed or cried or shouted. I simply needed more of Jesus. And like Sarah when Isaac was born, I felt the Lord was giving me laughter in place of sorrow.

So my spiritual search has come full circle. The Lord has allowed me to survive many attempts of Satan to rob me of my blessing, including the leaven of Pharisaism that almost caused me to miss Him. The flame of love I felt for the Lord Jesus Christ as a childish convert is being fanned into full-blown fire as I surrender to soaking prayer. I am beginning to learn what it means to be filled continually with the Holy Spirit (see Ephesians 5:18–20).

Pharisaism on any level robs you of what is really from God. It is an ugly substitute for true spirituality—a counterfeit you do not even know is there until you have tasted what is real. Then, recognizing what is real is only part of the battle. The wise man seeks until he finds and keeps himself flexible so as not to miss God.

Don't Miss *Your* Day

Almost a year ago, a picture came into my mind. It was as if Jesus were standing at the door of my house. Like a repairman, He was wearing boots and was laden down with tools and repair equipment. My living room in this mental picture was covered with brand-new neutral-colored carpeting. I had the impulse to put plastic down so the Lord would not step all over my new carpeting with His boots. I wanted to instruct Him where He could step and where I wished He would not. Suddenly I realized what I was doing: I was presuming to tell the Lord of glory what He could and could not do in His own house!

Jesus may be standing at your door right now. He is probably ready to fix some things in your life and church. Do you have the impulse to preserve appearances rather than let Him come in and do things His way, possibly leaving tracks on your new carpet? Or are you desperate enough to want Him, even if the evidence that He has been there includes a few footprints?

In order not to miss the day of God's visitation, open the door of your life and become flexible enough to allow Him to make the changes He wants. We are in days of renewal in the Church that are preceding a harvest so great that there will hardly be room to contain it. God is reviving the workers to gather in the harvest. The chief enemy of the Holy Spirit's work is Pharisaism. Whenever it is allowed to remain in any area of the human heart, it has the capacity to quench the Spirit's love and power flowing through us.

Won't you ask Jesus Christ for more of His love and power today, and full freedom from the binding power of legalism?

"Heavenly Father, make me more like Jesus and less like a Pharisee. Cleanse me from the leaven of legalism. Fill me with Your love and power. Give me the grace to love You more and to love others as You do. Let me see and experience the day of visitation You have planned for me. In Jesus' name. Amen."

BIBLIOGRAPHY

Beyer, Lisa. "Crazy? Hey, You Never Know." *Time*, April 17, 1995: p. 22.

Bible Illustrator. Parsons Technology, Inc., 1990.

Chevreau, Guy. *Catch the Fire.* Toronto: HarperPerennial, 1994.

Compton's Interactive Encyclopedia. Compton's NewMedia, Inc., 1993.

Grolier's Encyclopedia. Grolier Electronic Publishing, Inc., 1993.

Deere, Jack. *Surprised by the Power of the Spirit.* Grand Rapids: Zondervan Publishing House, 1993.

Dixon, Dr. Patrick. *Signs of Revival.* Eastborne, East Sussex, Great Britain: Kingsway Publications, Ltd., 1994.

Edersheim, Alfred. *The Life and Times of Jesus the Messiah.* Grand Rapids: William B. Eerdmans Publishing Co., 1971.

Edwards, Jonathan. *Jonathan Edwards on Revival.* Carlisle, Pa.: Banner of Truth Trust, 1994.

Gregory, Dr. Joel. *Too Great a Temptation: The Seductive Power of America's Super Church.* Fort Worth: The Summit Group, 1994.

Hall, Dudley. "Mercy or Sacrifice: From the Pit of Legalism." *Charisma*, April 1993: pp. 41–47.

Schaeffer, Dr. Francis. "The Mark of the Christian." *Christianity Today*, March 6, 1995: p. 29.

Seamands, Dr. David. *Healing Grace: Freedom from the Performance Trap.* Wheaton, Ill.: Victor Books, 1988.

Smith, William. *A Dictionary of the Bible.* Eds. F. N. and M. A. Peloubet. Grand Rapids: Zondervan Publishing House, Regency Reference Library, 1948.

The Revell Bible Dictionary. Ed. Lawrence O. Richards, Ph.D. Old Tappan, N.J.: Fleming H. Revell Co., 1990.

You may contact Melinda Fish by writing:

Church of the Risen Saviour
330 Edgewood Ave.
Trafford, PA 15085